CI

MW01601588

CLAIRVOYANCE

A SYSTEM OF PHILOSOPHY

First Edition 1897
J.C.F. Grumbine

New Edition 2019
Edited by Tarl Warwick

COPYRIGHT AND DISCLAIMER

FOREWORD

Grumbine's "Clairvoyance" is helpfully arranged into sections (or lessons) each with some simplistic experiments involved, all marketed under the concept of being a technically Rosicrucian work, released by the Order of the White Rose. The author was somewhat prolific and released a number of works which are technically how-to works, as this one is.

The content here is somewhat philosophical as well; at times it alludes to and quotes Jesus Christ among other individuals, and combines the strictly physical side of focus and mindfulness with a spiritual side which is more abstract in nature.

Hypnotism, magnetism, and trance states are also spoken of here; in the era in which this work was created, such topics were considered twain with the spiritual by many, as they were less well understood than in the present, and/or novel.

This edition of "Clairvoyance" has been carefully edited for format and content. Care has been taken to retain all original intent and meaning.

CLAIRVOYANCE

PUBLISHER'S NOTE

This work is both novel and unique in its subject matter as well as in the treatment of it. It is original, inasmuch as it marks a new era in metaphysics and spiritual science. It is a book within a book. It is one of a series of Teachings which form, as the author sees fit to name it, a "System of Philosophy Concerning Divinity" of which Psychometry is the first series, Clairvoyance the second, Inspiration the third and Psychopathy the fourth. Collectively, they establish a Rationale of Divinity. The author claims to be a seer; and while the philosophy herein declared and taught will satisfy the needs of those who recognize spirit, the spiritual nature and life of the world, its merits will and must stand the test of that invisible yet omnipotent Guide which shapes civilization and evolves consciousness.

There is a growing faith in the Divinity of man and its potential functions. Supernaturalism as theologically conceived is scientifically absurd, but re-defined literally, that is, given a spiritual and not a dogmatic interpretation, signifies the depth of a rational perception of Nature's forces and her unchanging law. Phenomena and noumena are correlative and coexistent in the sphere of causality. All is law, the embodiment and expression of law. The time will come when churchmen, like Professor Drummond and Lyman Abbott, will not be sacrificed upon the altar where the saintly Son of Man inspired their works in his name. England has paid dearly, she will yet pay more dearly, for the blood of a consecrated liberalism. The wine press is still red with the fruitage of a fading century and the new age is framing a cross on Golgotha for the prophets of the future generations. Still the Voice in the Wilderness will not cease its celestial monotone. The prophet has his career, he must sow the seed, whatever the world may care for the harvest. It is destiny, it is Divinity.

Speaking of this omnipresent law of the human consciousness, a reformer of note has written: "The inspired men are fewer. Whence their emanation, where and how they got their power, and by what rule they lived, moved, and had their being, we know not. There is no explication to their lives. They rose from shadow and they went in mist. We see them, feel them, but we know them not. They came, God's word upon their lips; they did their office, God's mantle about them; and they passed away, God's holy light between the world and them, leaving behind a memory, half mortal and half myth. From first to last they were the creations of some special Providence, baffling the wit of man to fathom, defeating the machinations of the world, the flesh and the devil, and, their work done, passing from the scene as mysteriously as they had come upon it." So is it, and so it will ever be, while their vision and works leaven and idealize society. It is this law which the author of this book seeks to make clear and, quite naturally, to prove that man is the oracle of the Divine Presence.

The reason why this book was published first is that it is less technical and will prepare the student for the other volumes of this remarkable System of Divinity.

CLAIRVOYANCE

INTRODUCTION

These Teachings constitute one of a series. It forms a rationale or system of instruction for the unfoldment of the spiritual gift (the natural endowment of all souls), commonly designated Clairvoyance. This System of Philosophy is the simple solution of the mooted question of human clairvoyance. These Teachings are neither abnormal nor supernatural in origin, nor are they to be regarded as unnatural. They appeal to the reason and are the corollary of Nature's Law and Causation.

Inspiration may be misunderstood, even denied, yet it is the most natural force in the world. Were it otherwise, it could not be. All thought is inspirational in character, source and end, and when truly analyzed establishes not only an *a priori* knowledge but the eternality of soul. Thought really is spirit vibration, and has its source, not in the brain, nor in any of its agencies or subordinate instrumentalities, but in spirit. To understand this, it must be realized that even organism has its origin in spirit This we can both affirm and prove, for the soul is the basis, as it is the law, of all its functions. Organism and organs presuppose their spiritual prototype. Man as an entity, immured in matter, is to be analyzed spiritually as well as materially; he is to be considered, not as an inverted pyramid, but in his true relation to what he is, as well as what he manifests, that is, what is externalized. Organism is what it is, because soul is what it is. Never is man what he is because organism is what it is. Spirit, the organizer and seat of intelligence, makes not only organism but organization possible. Thus the brain is acted upon, never does it act per se. Thus organism obeys, never does it govern spirit. The brain demonstrates the existence of spirit, not its evolution or involution. Its office is to manifest spirit as a mirror reflects the image of a form. In itself it is nonexistent, non-creative, nonevolutionary. Thought shines through it as light through a lens. The brain neither creates nor produces thought- it but reflects it.

Thought as the effect of spirit is twofold in its mode of manifestation. Always remember it is from spirit, whether the spirit be on this plane or another, incarnate or excarnate, as these words are generically understood. Experience is thought realization. It is more than demonstration. Tuition is experience; intuition is inspiration. Tuition is inspiration realized. A line of demarcation should be drawn between intuition and inspiration as universally or philosophically interpreted and understood. Intuition is the source of truth from within- this we designate Divine Inspiration. Inspiration is thought from a spirit or from spirits in or out of the material form. When in the mortal form such inspiration may be called telepathy or thought transference, and is often induced by hypnotism. When not so induced, it is the direct or indirect transference of thought from plane to plane, through medial and harmonial conditions.

That inspiration is possible to-day, as it was demonstrable throughout the history of the past, evidence of a various kind could be cited, all of which is unnecessary when the source of thought as interpreted by the true System of Divinity is fully understood. To Our Beloved Classes Throughout the World: Beloved Ones: To you we extend our greetings. We meet you, as it were, across the silvery ocean of this life, beyond the valley of the shadow of death on this side of immortal life, not as strangers or sojourners in a strange land, but as those who feel the kinship of spirit, who have awakened to the law of life and soul, and who realize that time and space, nor life or death, nor principality, height or depth, can separate spirits. In this sacred marriage of our spiritual natures by aspiration and spirituality, by spheres and planes of reciprocal love, we are one, though seemingly disassociated and separated by death. We stand within the veil, ever drawn to you, our love for you and our devotion to the cause of Humanity, our consecration to the Supreme Good, as firm and persistent as when in the earth life. We played amid the shadows of the outward world as you now do and we listened to the music of the spheres as Nature vibrated it. Step by step, our unfoldment was realized, but little did we dream that every act, as every thread in the shuttle that moves to and fro in the loom of life, formed the character of our spiritual being. This is the lesson of error,the aim of evil, that, possessed of being, the soul should rise into its final expression, its apotheosis.

The exercise of each organ, nerve, function, sense, faculty, perception of being, is for one purpose. All subordinate or collateral aims pay tribute to this purpose. It shines as the day star when all other orbs of light are destroyed. It towers as a flame, unquenchable and divine, when all other fires within the bosom are extinguished. It attracts as it fashions the soul in every plane and sphere, and it is the light that lighteth everyone that cometh into the world, It is the light of Divinity that unrolls the shadows of life and death, truth and error, love and evil, in relative spheres of expression. It is the interpretation of the unchanging Law, of the Logos of religion, of the unspoken words of Mystics, of the knowledge of Science. It is, it governs Being. It is the Will of God. All success, material and spiritual, must be one with it or they fail in their ideals. No superficial planes or height of being will avail to make it other than a consuming flame when shadows play in its aureole. Civilization, progress, history, are measured by it. It is the absolute standard of light. As science is evidenced by demonstration, so consciousness in its sphere of realization expresses the truth, this law, this apotheosis. As all drops of rain, as all springs, creeks and rivers are subject to the law of specific gravity of their elements and all tend to equipoise, so souls, in segregation and schools, move toward one end and one affinitization. Reality dictates the modes of spirit and psychic manifestation and expression. Life in every plane and sphere is harmonial and the exact illustration of the numerals in mathematical relations. Geometry is the exponent of the soul's progress in the light of the square, triangle, star or double triangle and circle. Thus matter serves spirit and both reflect and obey the law that geometrizes mathematics. Mathematics illustrates Religion as Science evidences Inspiration. When either mathematics or inspiration are comprehended, or when their law of relation is perceived, the conflict between spirit and matter, religion and science, spiritualism and materialism, is at an end, their integrity of essence and form will then be perceived and established.

All thought in forms of tuition, intuition and inspiration, in outward symbols of manifestation and realization, are predicates of the soul's progress. Progress means "literally going in," and the path of life is literally a going in from the night of ignorance and unconsciousness (and we use the word as expressing a degree of light and knowledge) into the day of truth, and hence illumination or the attainment of Divinity or soul realization. Thus manifestation and expression of spirit are for this purpose and this purpose only. Culture must then be radical, spiritual, as well as artistic, social and political, if it shall fulfill the end of Being. Education must be comprehensive, must include the science of the soul as well as matter, must include the philosophy of inspiration, as spiritualism teaches and reveals it, as well as sensuous knowledge, it must reach in as well as out for the surpassing light of Ra, if it is to lead mankind to a real height or an absolute attainment of spirit. To exist is not to live, as to die is not to reach oblivion or Heaven. Life is consciousness of duty and of duty obeyed and done. Thus all efforts for unfoldment should advance the spirit one degree nearer to deity. Thus, all attempt to confer with the denizens of another world should be for higher understanding of the Law of Being. Thus, every desire for spiritual or medial advancement, for the practical understanding and use of mediumship, whether of the mental or material character, should be for the purpose of leading mankind to a knowledge of the truth.

And as we draw near to you through these, our inspirations, we would impress upon your minds the necessity of thus co-laboring with us, that as light illumines you, so may it reflect unto others, that it may not come to pass in this century, as it was written of the first when the humble Nazarene walked the earth, "The light shone into the darkness but the darkness apprehended it not;" rather, that it may be said of you, "The exceeding glory of the light shone all about them, so that men felt it to be good to be with them."

This is the light which is revealed in the unfoldment of clairvoyance the science and philosophy of which we shall seek to teach you. Enter the temple of the spirit without fear, with clean hearts, and bow at the shrine where Love dictates her inspirations, and as each lesson is given to you accept of its inspirations and gradually the scales will fall from your outward eyes and the veil that conceals the spirit of your loved ones, even the angels, will be rent asunder, and you will be permitted to walk and talk with them. May "White Rose" teach you that angel love will lead you from above as it will inspire you from within until all things are fulfilled. White Rose, the Guiding Inspiration.

CLAIRVOYANCE

FIRST PRINCIPLES

Follow and obey them:

1. Tranquilize the spiritual, mental and material conditions by becoming at one with the spirit. This is attained by approaching the spirit in an aspirational or prayerful mood; by being receptive to inspirations as the earth is receptive to rays of light; by being passive or negative in spirit, viz., positive to spirit incarnate and vibrations which play in the sea of materiality, and negative to spirit excarnate and vibrations which play in the sea of ethereality; by being calm and restful, not impatient, anxious, worldly, selfish in your duty to the spirit. Prepare, as it were, a mental state as smooth and glassy and as unruffled and unmarred by contrary vibrations as the placid bosom of a lake. Thus on or into the mind, as a mirror, the image of thought through the process of clairvoyance will appear as the Guiding Spirit wishes.

2. The vision will be assisted in concentration by fixing the eye on a clear glass filled with clear water (aqua pura), and watching, as it were, the scenes that appear and disappear. This is simply suggested as an aid and not as a necessity for those whose minds are distracted and whose vision will not respond to the will or spirit Place the glass on a stand and have about it, when impressed, fresh flowers. Sit at least six feet from the stand. Change the water at each sitting.

3. Sit uniformly at stated times and place and three times a week, thirty minutes each time. Have the atmosphere in the room cool and fresh and free of all animal and vegetable impurities.

4. Sit in a dimly lighted room and alternate with total darkness. When sitting in the dark, correlate all impressions, that

is, subjective phenomena, with all manifestations, or objective phenomena, of the spirit. Observe the "lights," forms, faces, symbols, names, places, that are shown to you and watch the development or developing process through which you are taken. Note how conditions are prepared for the reflection of an idea in the mind and thence (through mind) on matter. Observe how faces, figures, etc., are formed out of the magnetic waves that play in your atmosphere and perceive how, by holding the thought, the spirits weave about it a form or image with which they clothe it, and which, when fully manifest, becomes an etherealization or a materialization.

5. Sit alone. Avoid promiscuous circles and influences. Sit with and follow the guidance of no media, lest your development be destroyed, the forces scattered and the guidance set at naught.

6. Sit when conditions can be best adapted to the work at hand. The morning or evening hours are the best.

7. Sit facing the East, that you may be in line with the spiritual or electrical wave currents which move eastward from the West. At night sleep with head to the North by East.

8. A very light lunch before retiring is allowed.

9. Be uniform in diet, sleep,, habits, recreations.

10. Pursue a vegetarian diet. Avoid, so far as it is possible, meats, stimulants, tobaccos, condiments, all greasy substances.

11. Live a pure, unselfish life, as spirituality has much to do with clairvoyance. It furnishes a clear atmosphere for the spirit and thus extends the range of vision by furnishing a

CLAIRVOYANCE

lucidity for definition and penetration.

12. Music is a valuable accessory and helps to bring about the necessary concentration.

13. As unfoldment means a gradual attainment of Divinity, clairvoyance is subject to the law that governs Divinity. Do not force results, but remember that though you are unaware, you through effort are reaching the end in view, and by holding the forces, and cooperating with (and not by grieving) the spirit, you will attain to that soul elevation where, as in a mirror, the spiritual universe will appear reflected. This will be neither a mirage of the vision nor a delusion of the senses, but a fact of Being. Go often with the Son of Man, the Teacher of Galilee, to the mountains and not only pray there but breathe the lessons of the heights.

14. Keep the body and clothes you wear clean.

15. During the process of unfoldment, go where the best music and lectures may be heard and where paintings and scenery of a high order may be seen. Above all, live a simple, natural life, and keep close to Mother Nature.

16. Read the best books on all subjects that lie within your sphere, and seek for knowledge everywhere. Mediumship, and its unfoldment, depend for its practice upon inspiration and education.

CLAIRVOYANCE

A WORD ABOUT THE EXPERIMENTS

It is not intended that the experiments which follow each lesson should be applied abstractly; rather, they should be tried in all conditions of life and environments, as they are susceptible to manifold variations and implications. They are both esoteric and exoteric in character and touch necessarily upon the field occupied by Psychometry. However, if the student will apply himself diligently to them, caring the most for successful results, and the least for predisposed prejudices as to their impracticability or for the antecedent condemnation of the Mother Grundys of both Physical, Social and Psychological Science or the *ipse dixit* of self-elected infallibility, that spirit of research and consecration will bring their rewards,

CLAIRVOYANCE

LESSON I

Clairvoyance: Its Definition and Office

In this series of Teachings we shall not attempt nor seek to effect the impossible. We are aware that clairvoyance, together with every other gift of the spirit, is the natural possession of all beings; we are aware that, whatever may be its definition or office, it has a place in the domain or Nature, as is attested by the history of the alleged "miraculous"; we are aware that though it is a faculty or possession of the mind denied by the agnostic and material scientist on the general ground that spirit as such has no existence separable from brain or organism (which position has been proven false by the recent phenomena of hypnotism, mind reading and telepathy); yet we maintain that clairvoyance is the natural seeing of all creatures. The seemingly Strange and inexplicable phenomena of clairvoyance, though repudiated by certain scientists as the result of abnormal action of the mind or as the effect of hallucination and hysteria, have made a very profound impression on a more earnest class of scientists, who, like the eminent Prof. Alfred Wallace, Crookes, Zollner and others, have applied an intuitive test, nay, have applied even a material test, and found them to belong to a psychic realm, in short, found them to be just what they purported to be. The mental as well as the physical phases or forms of the spiritual manifestations respond to their specific tests and prove by so doing their sphere or place in the range of Nature's phenomena. The Spirit, whatever may be the hypothesis of its origin or composition, is one of Nature's possessions, and by this we mean, it, as truly as any so-called elements, has a sphere in the universe and is explicable by her unchanging law.

By Nature, we mean the realm inclusive of all forms of life. Spirit demonstrates its being as well as powers through the

15

medium of Nature, and in the sea of her causation or law, it expresses itself. Whatever may be its wonderful and eternal endowment, Nature receives the reflection of it in her realm of causes and effects. She is the sea in which spirit swims, as ether is the medium that permeates all matter, and into this sea, as a mirror, the spirit reveals itself. The subtle and indivisible consciousness, inexplicable to both the scientist and philosopher, manifests here in Nature with no less concern for and obedience to Law as the elementary compositions of matter and force. Psychology, as well as physics, belongs to Nature and her processes, and there is naught anywhere in the domain of being that is not comprehended by Nature. This being at once admitted and true, the difficulty in the way of a clear and perfect understanding of spirit in the sphere and light of its phenomena has been, first, the limitations which men of science or theology put to Nature and the ability of Nature to reveal or manifest spirit through her processes, and, secondly, the lack of perception of the interior workings or divine immanency which establishes the phenomenal world in and on the noumenal world. That there is uniform causation in Nature, or that Nature herself must be uniform in her causation, follows the rejection of the alleged supernatural or interposition or interference of Deity; and that such is the natural order, experience and knowledge prove; but, that in the consideration of causation, however uniform, where there is unchanging law, science or theology should affirm the impossibility of spirit power as spiritual manifestations exhibit it, that it is no part and corollary of this causation, is unquestionably presumptuous, if not prejudicial in the extreme. Spirit may copy or plagiarize the uniform causation in its own laboratories where, as in seances for the display of all kinds of materialization, spirit excarnate repeat them by processes both chemical and natural, though subtler and finer in sphere and action, just as a chemist recombines the elements of hydrogen, sulfur and oxygen into a formula of sulfuric acid, or in a more simple way combines hydrogen and oxygen to form water. This we call copying or plagiarizing Nature. The elements exist and cannot be recreated by any spirit incarnate or excarnate, but through a knowledge of Nature, her law and processes spirit can combine and recombine by Nature's own formula what is eternal and inherent in herself. So, in like manner, the spiritual manifestations of the seance room which bear a likeness to the forms of Nature in the garden of the earth compare really with all physical phenomena of Nature, inasmuch as they are fashioned after them, are, in plain words, materialized and de-materialized by compliance with her law. It takes spirit on either plane to affect the result. The question which we shall ask the materialist to answer is, what does he know of Nature per se, or beyond the horizon of visible causes and effects which he terms Nature? He knows absolutely nothing. Without access to the knowledge which inspiration, intuition or the so-called dead give, he sees, as he examines, but the hemisphere of the universe, one and that the shadowy or phenomenal side of life. He knows naught of another world or form of life beyond the change called death. He doubts, he denies, he condemns all such affirmation of knowledge on the part of his equally wise, perhaps wiser opponent, and with ignorance and denial as his weapons, he seeks to answer intelligently the above question. We hold that he has no right to attempt to answer the question at all without investigating the grounds of his opponent, and then not, unless, freed from pride and prejudice, he will accept what is demonstrable to his reason.

And what we here say concerning the material forms of the spiritual phenomena, plagiarized from Nature by excarnate spirit in the seance room of media, is equally true of the higher order of phenomena, the mental, such as clairvoyance and clairaudience, which are but kinds of the same phenomena of spirit, are explicable by law. Seeing and hearing spiritually is not impossible when it is remembered that it is the only kind of seeing and hearing that is possible; but when even the seeing or hearing becomes inexplicable by the formula of science, when it must be accounted for by a causation, larger and more comprehensive than that of the books of the Royal Academy of Science, even then, it is none the less natural, none the less within the domain of Nature, none the less the effect of causation. The fact is, the word causation, as the word God, has been made a fetish and an unalterable and immovable concept of human understanding, whereas, the growing mind of man has given it each day and year a larger and more inclusive realm of definition. Mankind no longer accepts but rejects the mythology of the Israelites, Greeks, Romans, Hindus, Indians, but religion has not become less a fact by the disintegration and destruction of fetishism. So, also, in the realm of science and philosophy, systems of thought have been devised by noble minds and each created a concept or formula of truth, yet larger and deeper, seemingly, grew the ocean of truth as each life touched its waters. The ocean received the river of each one's thoughts, but lost apparently not an atom of itself. So to this same causation we turn for the definition and interpretation of clairvoyance.

And, possessed of its facts or phenomena, you have a right to reject any system of religion, science, or philosophy that first repudiates them and then denies clairvoyance as manifest, demonstrated and established by them; so that there should be no barrier to progress in the accumulation of knowledge and the freedom of the soul's life and expression of thought. This is the true scientific spirit that should characterize our attitude to truth and demand a conformity, not to obsolete formulas of science or theology, but to facts, a readjustment of thought and thinking to the truth that must now as always shape its present and future definitions. Clairvoyance is really, by definition, clear seeing. It is the awakened and awakening consciousness, and as such comprehends all that is designated by eyes, senses, faculties, intuition, mind and spirit. Among the Greeks it was likened to Apollo, who bore the flame of Jove around the world in a torch of piercing light, and by the Egyptians it was likened to the all-seeing eye that never slept. Consciousness, as we here designate clairvoyance, is the most inclusive synonym that could possibly be employed to illustrate "seeing;" for between seeing and perceiving, or "seeing through" anything, there is but a slight shade of difference of thought or meaning. To see anything, as the phrase is commonly used, is to see the outward form or proportions, and thus to understand the superficial definition; to see through anything is to see it not only in outward form but in essence, or as it is, and thus to perceive it and receive a true conception or definition of it. Seeing thus leads to perceiving, and may be called the means whereby one sees. Yet what we here teach concerning seeing in contradistinction to perceiving must not be given a literal signification, but it must be taken in the broad, spiritual sense. Seeing is instrumental to perceiving, so far as material things, that is, the forms of entities, are concerned, but mind, spirit, soul, is basic to all seeing or perceiving. Organically the eye serves the so-called sense of sight; the sense of sight serves the mind; the mind serves spirit, and the spirit serves the soul in all that outworks destiny. The spirit is seemingly duplex and reflex in character and action, and by this we mean it is concerned with the objective and subjective realm of life. The objective is comprehended by the material and the subjective by the spiritual universe. The spirit thus constituted receives upon its lens, the mind impressions from these two realms and it perceives them, according to its lucidity or ability to realize them. Thus, while impressions from the spiritual universe are constantly impinging on the mind, just as impressions from the material universe are floating in through the organ of the eye or sense of sight or feeling (for the veritable blind can "see" by feeling and thus form definitions of objects), few, indeed, are able to define such impressions or realize them as such, or even draw a line of demarcation between those that enter from the objective and those that enter from the subjective realm. This is due to the fact that mortals have not been so trained as to analyze impressions, or it is because of false theories of consciousness and false psychologies; thus they have regarded the mind or outward consciousness as the factor of sensation and thought, and have been concerned only with what is external, the objective or material realm of life. Cognition has as a result been limited by the necessity of the case to sensuous knowledge, and the ocean of inspiration has been regarded as a mirage of the mind, having no real existence in the desert of earth forms and life; whereas this very ocean is causal and fundamental to all that proceeds from or recedes into it. This character of the spirit or mind being once recognized, more careful attention and scrutiny can be given to all that manifests itself in it, and, more than this, a most perfect scope and definition of consciousness and the far-reaching extent of clairvoyance can be had. The objective and subjective realm are one in one perfect correlation and integrity of law. As each atom rotates on its axis in obedience to the law that revolves the planet earth and establishes the polarity of the sun, yet serves a purpose in its own sphere of action and serves it without mar or jar, so the mind acts in this twofold manner obedient to the principles that establish soul. If a definition of the forms of things as materially understood can be had through mind and the outward vision or sense of sight, surely a definition of the forms of things as spiritually understood can be had through mind and the inward vision or consciousness.

If spirit is the eye that sees and perceives, then it has access to its own realm, that of spirit in the objective and subjective sense and form. This is self-evident and follows the admission that the spiritual universe is (as the facts of life, of spirit excarnate prove).

This consciousness is the center of thought radiation where impressions meet and where they are perceived and received. This fact must be understood in the very beginning of our Teachings and the relation and principle of it thoroughly

20

mastered or what will follow will be ambiguous and confusing. The mind is a lens of the spirit, but it is spiritual in its character and composition, more so than the sensory, as the organ of the eye is the material lens of the mind. Consciousness, in the final or absolute sense, bears just such an intermediary relation to its various subordinate lenses in the organism of soul. We teach that the soul is the primate or basis of all organism, and when this is understood in the highest sense, it cannot be said that the material form of organism does not bear a relation to organism in itself or as a function of soul. The type is the basis; it establishes all of its forms which are but its manifestations, and from it as to it proceed the multiplicity of relations which form the network or chain of its operations. The system of muscles, veins, nerves, might, in an organic sense, be construed to be complete, if you begin from primates, as brain, will, spirit, or the functions of brain, such as the sensory, nerves, and heart, for which they stand; yet they are correlated in order of form to the type which more really approaches and bears a similitude to organism as spiritually comprehended. Neither of them could act independently, and yet each one does an independent work. Neither of them could exist in the spirit independently, and yet each has a specific office and work in the divine arrangement.

So, in this way, a similar congruity and harmony of relation and action exist between the organ eye, the sense of vision and the sensory where the sensations of outward visions are collected, and the mind, spirit and soul, in the consciousness which is the basis of them all; and the prototype is found in the spiritual counterpart which is, at once and simultaneously in action, the original basis of them. Thus, from the center of soul, the consciousness opens the mystic all-seeing eye, veiled by the arrangement which is defined by materiality or material expression. Now could you see in the real sense, the need of the eye, senses and mind would prove useless, but inasmuch as consciousness is awakened by the process through which you pass, in seeing, seeing thus through eyes, senses and mind, you become aware of yourself to that degree that you are able to rise above or to dispense with them. By this we mean, you cease to use them or they have served their office organically and functionally when the greater consciousness has appeared and you, with the consciousness that you have unfolded or realized, cease to utilize what is no longer helpful or necessary. Think of a germ employing a sheaf or shell or chrysalis out of which, as from a sepulcher, the life rises into a resurrection of new and higher forms of manifestation.

Think of a man clinging to the mind of childhood, after a higher and deeper consciousness has unfolded through the use of this same infantile mind; think of a bird going back into the shell, after its wings have cut the air, and its eye has caught the light of day; think of the soul sighing to reenter the womb of generating forms, after it has kissed the face of parent and received the caress of love from the denizens of earth and heaven. So, in like manner, not lost, but consumed, not neglected, but utilized, the soul enters through each form of organism, through even the mind and the spirit, into a clearer and more absolute state of consciousness and Divinity. The fact is, that in the process of evolution the mind with organism obeys the involution of soul. All order and life, in expression, proceed by impulses. Impulse is born of the principle that shapes the soul's apotheosis, and each impulse is in mathematical ratio to the other and in the succession of impulses, one order leads each and all. It is as the corpuscles of the blood that obey the beating or impulse of the heart, or the waves of the ocean or tides thereof that follow the impulse of the magnetic and electrical seas that influx the worlds. Not chaos, but order, is Nature's law. And as in each atom the impulse throbs obedient to that in the galaxy, so, in like manner, the will of God or Nature (as you please) shapes and vibrates all subordinate waves of motion that move to and fro in the loom of life. Thus the eye conforms not only to the impulse of the original type of consciousness (which is to be realized), but to that form of the type of consciousness, the mind, which now is; or, vice versa, consciousness conforms to the extreme limit of it in materiality, the eye, which sees because mind is in touch organically with it. The office of the eye is to serve soul in this effort to unfold consciousness. And in so doing, in seeing and then perceiving the definition of things in the objective and subjective realm, clairvoyance truly and really is attained.

We necessarily draw a line of demarcation between clairvoyance and mediumship and clairvoyance as here employed in the thought of the unfolded and unfolding consciousness; and yet, as there is no phase of clairvoyance which is not beautifully at one with and productive of consciousness in this sense of development or awakening, each has its place and serves a purpose. A clairvoyance which concerns the subjective realm, as a clairvoyance that concerns the objective realm, merely for outward definitions of forms of essence, is a clairvoyance of "seeing" but not a clairvoyance of "perceiving." Seeing is but beholding images of forms impressed upon the mind; perception is realizing the purpose; and if appropriated, it is gaining lucidity of consciousness, by which a clear vision of higher and more subtler spheres and planes of life may be realized. You are here advised to adhere strictly to this purpose of clairvoyance and to seek for the attainment and advancement of this interior consciousness wherein is revealed more than in the mind alone, which is changeable and which serves, as it awaits upon it, the surpassing light from within the soul, in which, as in the light of the outward sun, can be seen, not only forms of things, but their definition and principle of action, composition and relation, and by which the apotheosis may be reached. He that will climb to this height will be rewarded by the ethers that condition his attitude of vision and the view that stretches out before him, but he that loiters in the valley and will not ascend the mountain, who gazes at the heaven without and

CLAIRVOYANCE

within through the atmospheres that mar and befog his terrestrial and celestial vision, will miss the object of these Teachings. Clairvoyance will be the means of reaching the new heaven and the new earth within the realm designated by time and space and comprehended by the senses, but it will establish an altar and a shrine in each home where mortals may commune and where the angels, ministrant upon earth's children, may approach, that both thereby may receive the light and benediction of the skies, the cooperation of the spirit world all about us.

FIRST EXPERIMENT

Place the glass or goblet of clear, crystal water on the table. Become very passive and negative. Concentrate upon it and observe the pictures that manifest themselves. After the sitting note the same on paper and make comparisons with successive experiments. Be careful to note whether these pictures are from the objective or subjective realm.

CLAIRVOYANCE

Clairvoyance: Its Nature and Law of Manifestation

We have shown that consciousness in the sphere and light of clairvoyance and that clairvoyance in the sphere and light of consciousness are fundamental to a definition of being. We have sought to elucidate how as the consciousness is unfolded, both seeing and perceiving become more marked and extended, if not more penetrative and piercing in their respective spheres of action. What obtains in one sphere and plane of vision, so far as the nature of clairvoyance is concerned, obtains with precisely the same purpose in successive spheres and planes. There may be a variety of manifestations in the one mode or many modes of expression or unfoldment. Yet never do the manifestations outgrow the purpose of them, never does the expression exceed in sovereignty the end which it subserves. Invariable and immutable is the nature of clairvoyance, and this is at once the magnificent and wonderful attribute of consciousness, because this nature waits upon consciousness. What is true of optics, or the material science of seeing, is true of consciousness, and vice versa. Consciousness is spiritually constructed as the outward eye is materially, but on a far greater and deeper plan. There is no radical difference, but a similar relation between them. This must be so to insure or to establish perfect unity of action. As in mechanics, as is illustrated in machinery, there is a coordination existing between the principles of dynamics, generically understood, and the principles of instruments, between the principles of motion and the principles of agency or matter, and the brain or mind of man who invents the machine which is to serve him, as well as to be the field of his operation; so, between the eye, the brain and the mind, in the larger sphere of the spirit and soul, there is a unity of design, purpose and action. It has been assumed that if this is so, then the eye should reflect in materiality all that is potent in consciousness.

So it does, but scientists have excluded data which in psychology and spiritual science have declared an *a priori* knowledge and consciousness. Hence men in all periods of history, like doubting Thomas, have failed to grasp the spiritual or esoteric signification of such analogy. "Show us the Father," said doubting Thomas to Jesus, "and it sufficeth us." And the "I am in the Father and the Father in Me" still remains a mystery to the whole order of materialists, who, like Thomas, fail to perceive the divine immanency in matter or in man. Such must become transcendentalists before they reach a correct interpretation of spirit or matter in relation to each other. The design of consciousness is seen in each function or instrument which it uses, and as each function is a branch or part of the total mechanism or organism of the body, in which and through which the spirit operates, the material design and integrity are only perceived when correctly defined by and correlated to consciousness, which organism subserves as it foreshadows.

But the nature of the eye reveals the law that defines the nature of mind and consciousness. As in an apple, the nature of a part is that of the whole, and the apple is in maturity what it is in the fact of seed, or tree, so permeating the whole material frame of spirit, the nature of the consciousness is revealed. In this sense, the eye becomes at once the key to the nature of clairvoyance. For if in it or on it the nature of consciousness is manifest, then the purpose of consciousness, as we understand it, in the light of clairvoyance, will be perceived. Deeper and broader the vision may become, but the nature of it will remain unalterably the same. The eye is the citadel where "you," the personality, is posited to receive the impressions which play upon and enter your sphere or vision. You see and perceive them, and in so doing, reveal the nature of spirit and consciousness in the light of clairvoyance. Two conditions enter into the ability of seeing, in the objective and subjective realms, in the material and spiritual universe. The first is "light" in the material, and, second, light in the spiritual sense. The organ of seeing, the eye, has no ability to see in itself; for if it had there would be no need of mind. It might, as a mirror or a placid lake, hold images of outward things in its myriad of lenses, but these would vanish with its own disintegration; but, even in such an instance, light is necessary for reflection. There is no reflection without light, which must give or make the reflection possible. Thus the eye could receive no image of outward things in darkness except darkness which is a form of light and holds concealed in it all definition of things. The light of the sun, moon and stars, or artificial light, is absolutely necessary for a material definition of things; and only where this light obtains can the mind cognize sensations which carry from the world of phenomena to the world of spirit the results of seeing. But, on the other hand, expose the inoperative organism of any person, the house vacated by the tenant, to the light of the sun, and when life is extinct the light of the world has. no message to the spirit. The transition of the spirit from mortal life puts an end, for the time, to both sensation and seeing, as literally understood, and this light, which makes a definition of things possible, has served its purpose, so far as this person is concerned. It bears no sensations to it. The body does not feel, though it may receive the ravages of disease, and while light plays about old and decaying forms, the life or spirit receives none of its potencies. It has reached a realm where the need of the light of sun, moon, stars and candles has ceased. Eliminate, if you can, in the problem of the soul's apotheosis, the mind as the lens of the spirit, upon which is impressed and through which are perceived the sensations and images of sensations from the outward world, and light, as thus received, would fall as it does in the spaces about us, but, by virtue of the divine arrangement of the human frame to mind and spirit, not one ray of light is lost. As long as consciousness is maintained through the mind in organism, so long does the light from without serve its purpose. Some see little, others see more, as the degree of consciousness perceives, but the end is reached in all.

There is, however, a perfect and beautiful correlation and adaptability of rays of the light of soul to rays which are regarded as material in character and derived by chemical processes and combinations. For it is these rays of light from within the soul which, interblending with and correlating themselves to the material rays of light, that make "vision" or seeing at all possible. There is, then, the light of consciousness as well as the light of manifestation or matter. One rules phenomena and the material universe, the other spirit and the spiritual universe. In sphere of law and action both reveal the same nature. There is harmony existing between the eye and material rays of light, and the consciousness and the spiritual rays of light, and both are interlinear, that is, one in one and one in many and vice versa, in every plane and sphere of consciousness. For instance, a child, in approaching knowledge from without, sees outwardly in relations or definitions of things only that which the spiritual rays of light from within the soul give it to see.

In other words, though the whole world is lit by the light of the sun, it sees it but not to perceive it, and the latter occurs as the former only really when the perfection of the sphere of light within and without is attained. Thus experience waits upon inspiration and tuition upon intuition, and science upon revelation in the aeons of time and eternity. Thus the development or education of the child is from within outwardly, both in the seeing and perceiving of rays of light and what they define from and in both realms. This light of consciousness is the light that never was on land or sea, because it has its residence only in the soul, and must there be perceived and realized. It is

CLAIRVOYANCE

called the light of truth and to spirit excarnate it is the light of the spirit from within its own mystic realm. This light is the law of material light and dictates its phenomena. Its spectrum is uniformly the same. Its colors have the same signification. As there is one white light in both the material and spiritual universe, the nature of both are the same. Both interact harmoniously to reveal consciousness. This nature of clairvoyance of which we speak is the law of consciousness that makes clairvoyance the source or means of acquiring truth. If you would form two circles and in one place the sun at the center and in the other the spirit, through which the spiritual as in the other the material rays of light proceed, and make each degree a ray of light, paralleling the other in both circles, you would form a clearer notion of what we seek to teach by the inter-relation of the two forms of light.

Number one in the circle of the sun corresponds and interacts with number one in the circle of the spirit, and ever in mathematical ratio and geometrical progression. As the unchanging law destinates both circles, a turn from one toward two designates a higher unfoldment of consciousness; when number three hundred and sixty degrees is attained the spirit has ended its expression, it passes through the change called death and outworks other degrees in the succeeding circles of spirit. Be it not forgotten that one degree designates a circle in itself where spirit and matter interplay in this field of twofold light. The attainment of the soul's victory over matter is achieved in this transition in the circle of soul. Thus the manifestation of clairvoyance is obedient to this unchanging law which opens the vision as it deepens the consciousness, and which reveals inspiration and spiritual rays of light as earth spheres are utilized and states of consciousness realized. The law of clairvoyance is one of progressive seeing and perceiving according to our diagram, which, if esoterically understood, will become the formula for solving history and civilization.

CLAIRVOYANCE

SECOND EXPERIMENT

Sit in quiet concentration of spirit and form in your mind's eye an image of some one near and dear to you in spirit. Watch its formation and appearance and notice how it gradually becomes a spirit impression. Now, see, it clothes itself in the habiliments of spirit, and in the picture there are scenes presented. Try this experiment over and over and again and the transition from sense to spirit will be made and you will enter the realm of spirit at will.

CLAIRVOYANCE

LESSON III

Clairvoyance and Intuition Compared and Correlated

It is very necessary that the student of the spirit should have a clear and, so far as possible, a perfect definition of the relation which clairvoyance sustains to intuition. We have in a general way defined them as the "perceptions" of the spirit, but as this word is vague, ambiguous, and to some very misleading, it will be wise for us to make this word perception, as well as our definition of both clairvoyance and intuition, more absolute. In the first place, whatever human nature manifests, that the spirit reveals and possesses.

Naught can come through the mind or into the realm of mind, without originating first in the spirit. The type refers to the prototype and vice versa. Human nature by phrenologists has been designated a faculty and is said to occupy a special place in the frontal brain, closely associated with the perceptions. It comprehends the perceptions in the outward sense or use of the word and is closely allied with the vision, the individuality, the ego or entity. The fact is that in human nature, in this broad sense, the first gleam of the more occult consciousness came, for here, as it were, the angel of the skies prepared the way for and opened the door to the mystic realm of soul. In this department of mind the echo of the celestial voices first was heard and here the soul became aware, through both the subjective and objective form of spirit manifestations, of its own immortality. Human nature, however, is not a faculty. It is a term that faintly designates that nature which is one with, nay, is the identical consciousness or ego which has to do with the material universe in its subjective and objective forms. Mark, there is a subjective and objective side or character to both the spiritual and material universe, and, the soul has to do with both in the realm of consciousness. Objective refers to whatever belongs to ethereality or materiality and has to do with planes of inhabitation and expression, while subjective refers to spirituality and has to do with spheres of life or consciousness. Human nature is the extreme limit of consciousness, materially viewed, and is like consciousness duplex, so to speak, in its workings and character.

Could you, as an illustration, conceive of a mirror that could reflect what is within and without its own reflecting power, you would then have an idea of the power of the mind in general and of human nature in particular, as subjectively and objectively understood. Here in the realm of human nature the soul reaches out for the definition of reality and here it derives, by so doing, the definition of consciousness. Here it employs all that is potent in clairvoyance and intuition and at the same time shapes the objective by the subjective realization. In plain words, it derives by and through human nature the ability which is latent in consciousness and is expressed in the office of human nature, to enter deeper and still deeper into the uses and purposes of both clairvoyance and intuition. So that it comes to pass, in the natural evolution of human nature, as phrenology will attest, that such as are well developed in it are naturally both highly intuitive and clairvoyant, that is, they can exercise the more occult faculty of perceiving. We should guard the student from accepting too broad an interpretation of even this statement, for we do not mean that one who simply acquires by seeing a knowledge of the world is to that degree more perceptive, but we mean that as observation leads to generalization, and as a knowledge of one fact to a synthesis of many facts, so the changes in the mind take place, as the law of human nature is fulfilled. Human nature is a possession and refers to a state of the consciousness. It cannot be acquired by any artificial "learning" or adaptability to environments, but, though latent and dormant in all, it must be evolved by the same law that rules clairvoyance and intuition.

CLAIRVOYANCE

Some, indeed, may be deficient in it but efficient in clairvoyance and intuition, but this deficiency is due to the fact that human nature has fulfilled its mission and has given place to what is higher and more absolute. This is and will be so as the human race evolves a higher and at the same time a more spiritual consciousness and civilization. Nature avoids excesses and utilizes vacuum. She has no use for and need of any superfluity. Whatever in form has served its end in expression, that she at once disintegrates and destroys.

She adapts herself to the new conditions as spirit outworks the deeper and diviner consciousness. And as the end as well as tendency of evolution is toward synthesis or unity, from facts to truth, or from laws to law, so she hastens toward one in all her manifestation and expressions- one apotheosis. Means lead to ends and organism to consciousness in the idea of reality. Always, however, does reality in the consciousness dictate and outwork the end through the seemingly infinite variety of forms. Thus, as human nature reaches the sphere of clairvoyance or intuition, it ceases to be potent as such and yields to the sphere of vision and potency of Nature that it has attained. In other words, it becomes subject to a quicker and sublimer grade of vibrations and is impressed with a more instantaneous impingement of light from within, which gives it its action and seemingly independent regency. Let it not be forgotten that all spirit in the unfoldment of all grades and spheres of seeing and perceiving passed through the geography of human nature. It is in no sense true that highly intuitive and clairvoyant natures are such by a special dispensation of Divine Providence. God is no respecter of persons, and what is for one is for all and what is possessed or manifest by one can be and is to be manifested by all. Thus the unchanging law holds all in its sphere of Divinity. The fact is, the races of mankind follow a geometrical ratio of progression, and in this ratio the unknown quantity is really the most known, should be the most understood. Jesus, Socrates,

CLAIRVOYANCE

Appolonius, Buddha, Zoroaster, Hermes, all were apparently unknown quantities in the geometrical order of progression, for was it not said of them and as a proof of the saying were they not all persecuted and finally martyred: "They came to their own and their own received them not?"

Yet they were the known quantities to the seers, to those whose eyes were opened; they were the day star of the new age and generation, upon whose works the civilization of the future outwove her fairest revelations. Indeed, because this is so, the Divinity and deathlessness of consciousness are assured. These faculties are but the inlets to the ocean that vibrates within the limitations of organism, bearing to these outward shores of life argosies freighted with the golden fruitage of Eden bowers and filled with the sunlight of the inspirations of the Light of the World. And each faculty, as we designate it, ceases as such when the consciousness needs it no longer as an avenue for expression. Thus memory becomes an open book, in which the past, present and future can be read, when you have outgrown the use of it as defined by your prejudice of it. When you do not believe that it is allied thus to consciousness, when you limit it to the earth plane, when you make it and its office but a servant of your conscience and consciousness, then wonder not that the full potency and radiance of the all-seeing eye are denied you.

Herein, then, lies the mystery of perception, that embodied in and utilized by human nature; it unfolds its power and sphere as human nature serves its end; but its law is the law for all that follows it in the domain of consciousness. Perception is the word which designates the more interior faculty of seeing and has to do with realization. Human nature is the perception specialized, that is, embodied in a source of analysis based on observation. To perceive anything is to utilize human nature. Here the spirit derives its susceptibility to consciousness in the sphere of evolution.

CLAIRVOYANCE

Consciousness, as a quality of the soul, is as eternal as soul and is not produced by organism or the processes through which the soul becomes aware of it. But human nature and perception as thus used, the latter superseding the other in the order of faculties, and the former being a basis to the development and realization of the latter, are very closely affinitized to clairvoyance and intuition. Both are more interior in the realm of consciousness or soul and both are realized at a certain degree in the development of consciousness. Never is either human nature or perception, in the mind or soul, free of the cooperation and action of clairvoyance, in this sense, but as all seeing is clairvoyant, yet all perceiving is intuitive in character. However, there are degrees in the scale of unfoldment of both clairvoyance and intuition, and we here refer to this degree. It is one and the same in all. Each soul attains it when it touches it in the mystic circle. As all who travel to the sea-board can see the ocean, so all who arrive at this degree in the untoldment of consciousness behold clairvoyantly and perceive intuitively the new and wondrous sea of light all about them. We then are attempting no miracle when we send these Teachings to the world at this time, as the age is ready for them, as humanity is just emerging from the degree of human nature into the bright disk of the degree of clairvoyance and intuition and awaits this declaration of light.

Clairvoyance is, then, the clearer seeing as intuition is the clearer perceiving of truth in the objective and subjective realms. They refer to a more lucid and unfolded consciousness of soul. They lay hold of deeper and diviner relations of things. They see the unchanging law making inner as well as outer circles and perceive it, in its operations within, as on matter, within spirit and in the forms of it. We have designated intuition Divine Inspiration in contradistinction to inspiration through mediumship by spirits excarnate. As clairvoyance is seeing clearer, that is, with a deeper ken or penetration, due to the

CLAIRVOYANCE

unfolded consciousness and light from within, so intuition is perceiving, knowing or understanding, with a like ken or penetration, due to the same causes. And it is for each to know that consciousness is the door that leads to truth and love and to God, the solvent of all error and evil, the source of all light and power and peace from within its own realm of being. And beyond this it is for us to realize that this power of seeing and perceiving are possible with all, and that they are possessions of spirit, to be unfolded and utilized. A correct study and analysis of human nature and its office will confirm and affirm what we here teach and will lead to this realm where a clear definition of things can be had, because a higher knowledge can be received. Clairvoyance and intuition thus work in mutual reciprocity of sphere and aim, and lead the soul away from matter and the outward rays of light, away from reflections and shadows with all their entanglements, away from the quagmire of selfishness, into the realm of inspiration, where the light of God and the magnetic seas amid luminiferous ethers bring the vision and perception into a more perfect harmony with Divinity.

EXPERIMENT III

Do you realize any unfoldment of spirit as thus declared? Study well yourself and answer from the depths.

CLAIRVOYANCE

LESSON IV

Spirit Limited in Matter

There is no question but that "matter" as the word is generically understood means more than "materiality." It is not merely the stuff out of which is woven or fashioned the spirit's form and tabernacle, but it bears a relation, both subtle and occult, to the spirit in the law and purpose of its life and expression. Were it an entity, as some sophists seem to believe, it would at once usurp the sphere and office of spirit, and in it would be found the intelligence that moves and governs the world; on the contrary, it is not the entity, but the form or mode of the entity's being, and as such it is forever subject to the law and limitations of the entity. The so-called elements of matter which are regarded as unchanging and unchangeable, as spirit, are fixed in their chemical actions and affinities by the same law that governs spirit, and while matter is limited, spirit, by virtue of the unchanging law, is likewise limited. There are various degrees of limitation, in the order of expression; the word limitation is not to be given a literal but a spiritual interpretation, and matter in the light of limitation must ever be referred to spirit. We maintain that the elements, as we view them, have a spiritual as well as a material signification, and as the one is related to the other in the integrity of being, so in the one is the law of the other. Matter as materiality is subject to matter as ethereality, and if it be true, as chemistry alleges, that ether is the universal substance from which, as from a quarry, are mined the elements which compose the outward body of nature, differing from the crude only in the sense of sublimation, being governed by the same law, then the solvent of the body of Nature is in ether. But what is ether? Here the chemistry of earth is balked. It has no formulae, tools or appliances for penetrating the mystery of ether. Its vibrations are subtler, more sublime and spiritual than those of light.

Light can pass over and through ether without any apparent friction and without losing one degree of its quantity of force or momentum. It seems to be as a fixed mirror over which life's image can float without ripple or mar. And yet ethers respond to motion and vibrate by the same law that affects activity in all other planes and spheres of chemical or elementary forces. As a medium, it interpenetrates the interstices of all elements and is subject to conditions more inherent in itself and in spirit than in ethereality, one of its forms, or in matter, as materiality, a more basic or the base of all form. But we hold that matter, in forms of materiality and ethereality, outflow from ether, and ether is the reflection of entity. It has no existence per se. As time and space, which are alleged to be the properties of spirit, have no existence separable from spirit, as sweetness is a quality of essence, and has no existence in itself, so without reality ether would be unthinkable- it could have no existence. If this be true, then it follows that matter as illustrating ether also illustrates spirit, and in the material universe as in the spiritual universe can be found the fabric of soul. This fabric is the soul's wardrobe which belongs to it as much as any of its faculties.

Take, for instance, a spirit in its evolution. It first manifests itself in garments which are needful and harmoniously adapted to the state of consciousness which it expresses. Out of this state it weaves, so to speak, the subtle tissues that make up its material habiliments or vesture. These garments are its own, as this composite mass of matter, void and lifeless, so to speak, is its own, and having these elements allotted to it, by the law and integrity of being; the soul, expressing itself through them, in spheres and planes of involution and evolution, in the process toward the attainment of Divinity or apotheosis; it, with its form, according to the degree of consciousness it outworks, becomes gradually refined. The spirit has material as well as spiritual possessions, but not in the literal sense; it has property here as yonder in the skies. It has a right to all that its Divinity gives it, and no more and no less. And the beauty of the soul's apotheosis, in the thought of both the indestructibility and persistence of the material universe, as even the materialists teach, is in the fact of the preservation of its Divinity in all planes and spheres of expression. To possess anything is not to carry it with you in the form in which the possession is made apparent, but to really possess it is to have it in the sense of the good that it affords and to take the good as a worthy collateral. So when you possess a body in a material form and forfeit it by death, having outgrown and outlived its use, a collateral of it is restored to you in the form of the ethereal or spiritual body. This spiritual body is the prototype, nay, the harmonial counterpart, or correspondent, in spirit type, of the material body; and this finer body, which the excarnate spirit employs, is no less a possession, is no less the fashion of its personality, is no less a type of what will follow in the evolution of the soul as the earth form. Indeed, as the soul is to its consciousness in both planes of habitation, the body is to the spirit. In the first body of the spirit is the idea of the fundamental and ultimate personality.

In the first body of the spirit, as in the last, are found the same elements, in different degree of refinement and luminosity. Organism is the soul's instrumentality and it must be interpreted, spiritually or psychically, to be fully appreciated and understood. And this organism of soul inheres in all forms of it, throughout the sphere of the soul's expression. Nay, more than this, it defines as it establishes the character of the tabernacle that the spirit inhabits. Always is the lower order or form of organism conditioned by organism absolutely, and always in this ratio of planes, one, two, three, and so on, following like spheres of consciousness in the development of the soul, does organism reach the final type. Elements as ethers in forms, both material and spiritual, belong to the spirit and they are the spirit's property for reaching expression through manifestation. There is no more matter in crude than in fine, as there are no more ethers than souls to utilize them in the celestial life. For every spirit there is so much matter, and this matter is its property, and belongs to it forever. Upon this fact in the law of soul is established the science of Psychometry. This matter is referable to the soul and to the soul's type of personality, so that each soul attracts to it its own elements.

It never holds in its sphere of Divinity, although it may utilize, elements that belong to other souls. It can only use what the type of personality needs, and we might go so far as to say that every element has its psychic attractions and repulsions. This being so, the dream of life in matter brings its own interpretation. Consciousness is the law of the organization of the form. All elements tend toward psychic centers of attraction and repulsion. Polarity in one element moves toward a like polarity in the soul. Thus nature maintains an inerrant equilibrium and thus the balance is outstretched in all forms of life. The balance is the symbol of Divinity. It sits enthroned in mathematics which is the formula of the Cosmos. It rules the consciousness in its attractions and repulsions and it ordinates the ratios of planes and spheres. It makes the shadow alternate with the sunshine, and in the balance birth and death weigh expressions of life unendingly; so that the body of the entity may be designated the symbol of the soul's expression, and interprets the sphere of the soul's apotheosis.

The body is, plainly speaking, the condition of consciousness which is the state of the soul. Here is received and impressed the image, both human and divine. Here in materiality, the soul reaches the light of life, the impulse from Divinity, the inspiration of the God Principle, and here it outworks, in the laboratory of Nature, the personality in the light of the unchanging law. The body, as a condition, is, and must always and necessarily be, the reflex of the mind, the state of the consciousness of soul. In it in crude form is all that can and will be evolved. It is a photograph of a more interior and divine negative or image of soul; negative, because and when spiritualized, positive because and when materialized. Yet in the condition as is illustrated by the body, is the law of the state of consciousness of soul as is illustrated by the mind. Thus spirit is limited in matter and every faculty of spirit is thus circumscribed. This being so, it follows that the unfoldment of the spiritual perceptions is limited by this state of the consciousness, and that the body, in organism, leads to this inference. Consciousness is the symbol of the deific vision that knows neither the limitation of time nor space, perceives without seeing and is as the All Seeing Eye. And as there is evolved in consciousness the need of light, both as materially and spiritually understood, it follows that "knowledge through the senses" and "wisdom through the perceptions" are the inductive and deductive methods of its illumination. The vision of a mortal is limited by the natural conditions imposed upon it.

So, also, is the vision of a spirit excarnate limited and in like manner. Not only is this true, but it follows, that where the vision of a mortal and a spirit is limited by the same state of consciousness, all other conditions being equal, both are limited in their spheres of clairvoyance. The spirit cannot transcend the visual ray nor the clairvoyant penetration of a mortal, nor vice versa. But let it not be overlooked that not every such mortal utilizes or expresses to the fullest degree, his clairvoyance. And this may be likewise true of the spirit. But no degree of clairvoyance is denied a mortal, except that which is limited by the expression. As the expression is the all important end to be outwrought, the clairvoyance follows its order of development. All who are clairvoyant illustrate this aim or peculiarity. The knowledge which is a mortal's possession by intuition or inspiration is his as well when communicated by excarnate spirits. As a river cannot rise higher than its source, so consciousness cannot bring a knowledge beyond the natural perception of the spirit. Thus, what is received inspirationally under the guidance of the spirit can be received through intuition or the spiritual perceptions; and always is the former revelation one with the latter, according to the above principle. Thus, in the realm of cause and effect, a mortal follows an absolute law, the process of seeing and perceiving being one in all in harmonial spheres of consciousness.

That some organisms are specially adapted to the extensive exercise of clairvoyance does not, in any sense, disprove what is here affirmed. Mission is the purpose that souls fulfill and it refers to an adaptability to the end for which the person is called or sent. All have missions adapted to their peculiar sphere and plane of life, which are natural and divine. As seers or teachers, they are no more divine than common humanity. They, by virtue of their peculiar organism, which reflects a state of consciousness that evokes the office and mission of their work, find their place in life and become a Nemesis or Avatar of a new age or a new dispensation. And these beings are as likely to be called forth from the hovel as the palace, provided the spirit is prepared for the mission. Preparation is the all important qualification or prerequisite. None who have in them the aspiration for this clairvoyance should while away the hours in idle dreaming, but rationally and systematically unfold the spirit in this direction. No state of mind is fixed, for the expression of each age or cycle is so wonderful, comprehensive and universal, that the spiritual perceptions can be quickened and illuminated beyond all extravagant imagining.

If the object of development be to see and perceive, not only by means of mediumship, but through intuition and the mental establishment, then success will be the fruition of patient effort. The limitations of nature are placed upon the ignorant and

CLAIRVOYANCE

worldly or those who are wise in their own conceit, but the aspiring and trusting spirit, who approaches the light of inspiration, which is the light of clairvoyance, as a child, will not be denied access to the realms within or on high. Into the life of such the light of truth shines, that having eyes they may see and having ears they may hear, and having hearts they may understand what the spirit will declare to them. Aspire and toil for this surpassing light and the dawn of the endless day will break through the outward windows of the soul and bring in its radiant light a spiritual and clairvoyant vision both deep and divine, a revelation of symbols and spirit, of forms and reality.

EXPERIMENT IV

Fix your mind on a five-pointed star, and watch it in its kaleidoscope of colors and observe what takes place back of it. Observe this closely.

CLAIRVOYANCE

LESSON V

The Science of Optics Materially and Spiritually Considered

INTRODUCTION

The science of optics is not only the science of light but of seeing, as these words are both materially and spiritually understood. As the science of light is understood in relation to its phenomena, as its nature and source are still matters of conjecture and speculation, very little credence can or must be attached to the deductions of the natural philosopher. True, his doctrines and inferences are worthy of consideration and should be examined in the light of facts and reason, but no time-honored doctrine, no superstition of science, whether accepted by the generality of men of science or not, should have the precedence over the truth. There is no form of science, in any of the many departments of knowledge, which is not temporal in its inductions, and, hence, which does not illustrate relations. Forms or systems of truth change m the type of involution becomes a type of evolution. Forms serve the spirit of life and the thought of spirit; and in the progressive scale, a graduated form adapts itself to an unfolding thought, mind and spirit.

Thus civilization is the unique illustration and achievement of progressive forms of life as spirit incarnate, and these forms follow and obey the ratio of expressions that the soul fulfills in the life which is manifest in them. Thus, while one form has in it and reveals through it thought adapted to the spirit in its expression, yet it must not be received as a final type of the Logos. It should not become the fixed standard of measurement. It should not be regarded as infallible and absolute for all time to come, but, serving the purpose which it fulfills and the age in which it manifests, it should foreshadow and prototype the successive and preceding forms of thought. There is a relative and an absolute type of thought. The former is the manifestation, the latter is the logos or the will of God. Toward the fulfillment of the logos spirit, by means of unfoldment, in involution and evolution, is tending; this is the meaning of embodiment or incarnation, as it is the aim and signification of all re-embodiment, when a necessity. We do not imply that the science of 1800 B. C. or that of 1800 A. D. is not one in aim and sphere of form or definition, but we hold that in the thought of the mystic number one, illustrating the totality of all knowledge in its fractions and combinations, all that proceeds from it is subject to it, and that the relative can never be quite as final as the absolute, or as infallible as the truth itself. The evolution which is subject to the law of involution is always less than it, never greater, on the same ground that soul is greater than body, through which it operates. The word greater must here be given not a literal or comparative, but a spiritual definition. Thus, whatever science has revealed or achieved, whatever and however much we may know or perceive of the Logos, or the unchanging law, the Logos or law is greater than our knowledge, and by the fatality of our expression, the limitations of our understanding and perceptions, it dictates and leads us into the higher spheres of its presence. Be it so that science is one forever, because between knowledge and facts there can be no discrepancy, yet the circle shows an infinite relativity of configuration of souls, the degrees in each circle of expression, both materially and spiritually aspected, making a circle within the greater, the lesser one being subject to the law of the greater, and fulfilling a unity of design and purpose in both, truth ruling at the center of each and balancing all in one uniform and perfect motion or rhythm. Axioms are the postulates of science as materially considered, and in them are found, as upon them are built, the facts of the spirit's correspondences. Whatever science, through the human understanding, has discovered to be, that no age or generation outlives; but the relative is ever taking on and revealing the thought of the absolute, the Logos. Truth is ever absolute. Facts may change their plane of manifestation, but they never change their purpose, which is to manifest truth. One series of facts may be followed by another series in any one department of life, in biology, geology or chemistry, yet each bears an integral relation to the other, in sphere and plane of purpose and manifestation, and the unity of the order, in arithmetical progression, is never destroyed.

Ever does it reveal immutable law. Thus, the science of optics will suffer naught through additional revealments, for with facts as its collateral it must establish itself upon what is axiomatic or self-evident. What, then, if we should teach that the potency of light is in its spirituality and not materiality, and that the eye is not the seat of its recognition as the brain is not the source of its sensation? What if we should declare that without the spirit the light from without would be darkness to the brain? What if, after examining the claims of the materialist, we should affirm that the spirit, through its own light, parallels in materiality, nay, interblends, by a process beyond the analysis or understanding of man, its rays of light with the affinitizing rays of the sun, so that there is a sphere of light formed, in which the soul forever exists? What if we should affirm that these spheres are circles, radiant and transparent, in which consciousness is revealed and unfoldment is outworked from within essence?

What if, at last, we should declare that each soul has its spheres of darkness and light, as well as its spheres: of light and darkness, that have been utilized and exist only in the forms of consciousness, that have been fulfilled, but which are omnipresent? This is the purpose of this lesson. The spirit is the source of all finite light, as God is the source of it. It has its own light, which is as many times more radiant and clear than the sunlight as it is more luminous than its negative, the contrasting darkness. It is the light of essence, of being, of love. It is deific in

46

CLAIRVOYANCE

luminosity, differing from the light of God only in degree. Their quality is one. This light is colorless, but is, in the chemistry and media of earth, through prisms and the spectrum analysis, of seven colors, or three, in four complementary forms, making a uniform octave. These colors are red, yellow and blue, making the complement of four, orange, green, indigo, violet, and the seven in all. A perfect and proportionate interfusion of the three or the seven will produce the white, more or less pure as the colors and media are pure. As spirit is indefinable in form, so light is so in color. None of the seven colors or the three can truly define it. It is capable of refrangibility, but it, in itself, defies analysis. Thought has a like composition and is capable in the spiritual prisms of a like refrangibility, so that there are those teachers among us who hold that thought is light. As there is no light without thought and no thought without light- there is some ground for their inferences. We, however, hold that light is a quality of thought but is not thought. It is its atmosphere, potent and radiant as the thought is for good, but quite the reverse if for evil. All thought has its sphere of light and hence its degree of radiation. It interblends with like rays from all psychic centers. It correlates itself by an integrity or law of spheres to thought in all planes, and in uniform degrees of vibration. Material light, so called, is thus affined to spiritual light, with this difference in souls, that the particular ray is to the general what the general is to the particular; in plain words, one soul is to another soul in sphere and plane what one (I) sphere is to one (I) plane of souls.

As the sun is the source of material light and God is the source of spiritual light, souls live and move and have their being in both by an order and ratio of spheres and planes which are mathematically correlated and exact in both the material and spiritual universe. The outward ray that reaches the sensory responds to the inward ray that correlates itself to it, and when the fusion or union is formed, the sensation of light and thought is apprehended and defined. Perception follows a deeper light, and while it is subject to the same law, yet it is more interior and mystic in its operations. It works through lenses and apparatus that are so refined and spiritualized that no adequate conception of them can be formed or a definition or illustration given in the language of earth. The eye, the organ of vision and sense of sight form the cabinet where the forces, in the laboratory of spirit, are gathered and concentrated and where visions of things are "made up." Here the ego or spirit through the medium of the sense acts as a cabinet chemist, and, connecting the psychic with the material ray of light that enters the pupil of the eye, the outward curtain, through which the light enters, by the principle of expansion or contraction, the pupil becoming contracted when the light is strong, and expanded when weak, forms the necessary image or definition of the object that is conveyed on the outward ray.

The retina of the eye is the outer cabinet, a camera obscura, or a darkened chamber, where the outward or material rays are married to the spiritual rays from within. This retina or camera obscura is dark, not in the spiritual but the material sense, and for the same purpose that the cabinets for physical manifestations, through mediumship, are more or less darkened. The retina thus becomes negative to the positive, as the positive becomes negative to the rays of correlated light. The womb of life in all forms of organism is constructed on and operated by the same principle. Wherever generation of life forms or thought is to take place, the process is one and the same, the differentiation being in mode or process, not in principle. Darkness is a condition for generation. Life entering forms follows the same law that controls life entering thought spheres. Each spirit is born and reborn in this sense, from plane and sphere to plane and sphere forever. Here in the retina, the light of the spirit reaches the rays of light through the eye and from the outward sun, and they are not absorbed here, but rather they are fashioned into the form that is conveyed by the thought of the ray from within. The sense or sensory is the medium of translation. Here the form is given its spiritual type, its idea. And the significance of this is in the fact that only those outward forms are sensed that are received. Forms may be seen but not perceived, as we have elsewhere shown.

The spirit operates in this way, that the forms or definitions of outward things in the light of thought may be received. Afterward, as the inspiration dictates, as the mind is prepared to realize the materiality of the outward rays in the light of their spirituality, the perceptions are used and the ideas become realizations. And when this occurs, Nature will not repeat the phenomena. When one degree of the state of consciousness is attained, the consciousness passes toward the next and so on, until that phase of its expression is fulfilled. Then in the loom of soul the pattern makes a shift, the warp and woof silently await the action of the shuttle in its forward and backward movements, while consciousness receives the rays of light from within and without, which, when sensed and perceived, embody the purpose of the design. Each sense acts in this order and leads to this end. The brain is the central office where all the organs are kept moving in accord with the law of spirit.

The sense acts in perfect harmony with the organ, and as the medium between the brain and sensory it fulfills the office of the spirit, by connecting and translating by means of its mechanism the rays of correlated light. Strangely true is it that in both rays thought is conveyed, and most strangely true is it that an identical thought is revealed. The mind and brain act in unison with the spirit, and in the circle of these rays of light and thought all sensation as well as all definition of things, so far as the consciousness and perception of the spirit are concerned, are obtained. Thus the outward material ray is a hemisphere, and with the inward, spiritual ray makes a sphere or circle. You can become aware of this if you choose to analyze thought as vision and vision as thought from center to circumference. Errors are made when the connection is not perfect, through disharmonious and incongruous organic and psychic conditions. But the law of truth is also the law of error.

We maintain, then, that the real source of light and vision, as of sensation and thought, is in spirit, and that there is the provision for definition, perception, demonstration and realization. Thought is both positive and negative as materially and spiritually viewed. To spirit excarnate it is positive, as to spirit incarnate it is negative, and vice versa. To the outward mind of spirit, material light is positive, while to us it is negative, and vice versa. So in the divine, organic and psychic arrangement, spirit, in the formation of thought, generates it where the outward light is negatived by the spiritual light, which is positive, and, by such chemistry as is opposite in polarity and plane of operation from material chemistry, being subjective rather than objective, it develops material rays of light and all that is potent in them into their spiritual forms, so that they may be seen or manifested in consciousness. The mind is the field of the seance chamber, where the spirit reveals her formations or visions of ideas. And sometimes her forms or visions are crude, as the brain, mind and outward media are harmonized with the thought that is to be embodied.

For every spiritual ray of light from psychic realms, or for every thought, there is a material counterpart in the sphere of material light. There are no more rays of material than rays of spiritual light. Thus the unity and integrity of the cosmos are maintained amid a seeming chaos and confusion. All is law, order and harmony, even error and evil fulfilling the law of spirit.

The science of optics has this material and spiritual

CLAIRVOYANCE

signification, and it is within the province of science to demonstrate these facts which we have here declared.

FIFTH EXPERIMENT

If this be true, is it not as easy to see and perceive spiritual things as material, and if so, why then is not clairvoyance the gateway leading to the skies? Allow the spirit to gather up those rays of light which convey the visions celestial, observe and analyze what you see. Concentrate on the spirit and shut out from the mind and the eyes the solar rays of light. The mind will become the revelation of wondrous scenes and beings from the spirit world,.

CLAIRVOYANCE

LESSON VI

Vibrations: Their Law in Relation to Light and Sight

There is no question but that the science or law of vibration underlies the whole structure or organism of spirit.

Whatever is potent in the universe expresses the action of this law. Mankind are creatures of this law and with life and its myriad of forms share its regency and operation. This law is one with the unchanging law, to which we so often refer, and is a mode both of its action and interpretation. If we should affirm that the nature of the unchanging law is the law or mode of vibration, we doubtless should not be misunderstood, for the action of the unchanging law, however various and entangled in the meshes of planes and spheres, is the corollary of its vibration. Vibration is pulsation, movement, action, as may be illustrated in the lungs or heart or crudely in the delicate spring of a watch. It is the reiteration of force from one center of radiation to another, where action and reaction may be equal or unequal.

In momentum or intensity, vibration presupposes a center of radiation, from which it derives its momentum. Each essence in itself, as well as in its form, has such center of vibration, and while it is not apparent or understood, yet is it the cause of all that is designated the phenomena of life. There is what is called mechanical or dynamic and psychic vibration and the former is under the government of the latter. Vibration is the exponent or interpretation of exact science, of mathematics. It is in every plane and sphere of manifestation or operation the exact formula of the unchanging law. It is not senseless or unintelligent motion, but is the effect of cause, as intelligent as it is eternal. The trend of modern science bears happily upon this System of Teaching.

CLAIRVOYANCE

The tendency of materialism has been to divorce the dynamic from the psychic or spiritual on the ground that spirit is not existent as an essence or entity, and to trace in the program of uniform causation as illustrated in material physics, chemistry and biology the steps that lead to mind and spirit. And spirit thus became an evolution of matter and the product of it, always less and never greater than the elements and forces that evolved it. But the facts of spiritualism, both in the ancient and modern world, and the universal prevalence of the phenomena of clairvoyance, hypnotism, ghosts and magic of all kinds (not legerdemain) have turned the tide of thought to a more radical and opposite statement and interpretation of life. No one who is at all informed upon the subject denies that the phenomena of matter and force are under the government of law, but there is a various interpretation or definition of law. Scientists of the most ultra sort have been loath to make law and intelligence identical and they have been equally indisposed to externalize law. They have called it a process, a mode of action inherent in and indigenous to matter, and even where it seemed necessary for them to attribute to it at least the element of wisdom they have disposed of the difficulty by designating the process "evolution," making this word cover and explain all doubts and answer all difficulties. It is not to be denied but that this last resort is the confession of the weakness of their position and the triumph of the metaphysician. It is the *fin de siecle* of modern scientific research and it means everything for the spiritualist. For though the spiritualist does not confound law with intelligence, he makes law the mode of intelligence and thus is not driven to extreme and erroneous assumptions to account for the facts. We teach that as the unchanging law is the mode of spirit, natural and spiritual law or law that concerns spirit embodied and spirit disembodied, in materialty and ethereality respectively, are the phases of its manifestation in the material and spiritual universe.

The law is the same as a unit of radiation. The

so-called forces, as electricity and magnetism, are not laws, but conditions of matter, and they exhibit the action of the unchanging law in their respective spheres or planes. Of course, it must be remembered that the entity, whatever may be its name, is the source of intelligence, the seat of law, the center of all radiation; and the material forms and phenomena of life act obediently to the vibrations or radiations of the entity as here declared. Should you examine the vibrations of hydrogen or nitrogen, you would find that they are uniformly the same, each after its kind, because each element, so called, as a point of motion or radiation, depends upon the unchanging law for its vibration, as also it reflects and refracts the force and radiation given to it. Nay, more than this, the sphere of Nature may be likened to a body literally circumscribed and permeated by the unchanging law, where every atom, form, phenomenon of life, even life itself, is the illustration and exponent of the law.

Let us not be misunderstood. The law is the mode of the intelligence and illustrates it. Conscience and consciousness both obey the unchanging law, but for the entity the law is potent in all planes, and spheres of action. The law never changes its purpose. That purpose is fixed and absolute and destinates life in the form. The law as the mode of essence or soul of spirit, mind, life, of the much-abused words, consciousness and conscience, ordains and governs the planes of manifestation and expression. In other words, the ascent of life is ever toward the perception and realization of the unchanging law. It has a lesson for each plane and sphere of life and these lessons lead to higher interpretations and deeper understandings of the unchanging law. The integrity of the law is maintained forever and ever. A child is still soul and is still under the government of the unchanging law after it has outgrown or used the lessons of childhood. One sphere or more spheres of consciousness do not exhaust the resources nor fulfill the purpose of this law. The mode may have a variety of spheres of differentiation and yet be uniformly one in purpose and inclination. Light absolute is one in color and form though it has an apparently infinite differentiation. The ray of light is one on the surface of the sun or earth or through the media of prisms of ether. It loses naught of its potency or mission by vibration. Its mission is to vibrate at a uniform rate, always the same mathematically. So, the unchanging law is both absolute and relative in action and it is the spectrum where all life centers and radiates. This being so, as Nature in her manifestations and expressions of life evidences we have a key to the solution of the problem of clairvoyance. Light obeys the unchanging law in every plane and sphere of consciousness. Consciousness fixes the radiation or vibrations of light spiritual and material. In exact mathematical figures the vibration of light, in corresponding planes and spheres of consciousness, cannot here be stated, but suffice it to say that the consciousness through the brain radiates in exact harmony with the outward ray that weds itself to the inward ray through the action of the spirit. And these rays serve their purpose according to the principle of reflection and refraction. The eye and the brain, acting in harmony with the soul through the mind and spirit, receive the outward rays, not in their original intensity, but by the process and in the form of radiation and in the psychic as well as the organic apparatus, this interblending of the material and spiritual rays of light is affected. By means of this mystic process, the necessary vibrations of light are conformed to the spiritual vibrations and all ratios are fixed by the state of the soul which is to be outworked and fulfilled. Angles of declination and inclination play an important part in this process. Thus darkness serves its purpose as a mode of light where the vibrations are the least potent for spirituality but the most potent for materiality.

Thus evil and error are words which, when philosophically interpreted, are full of meaning and Divinity. Thus we find the angle of least inclination to the unchanging law where the lowest order of intelligence and spirituality obtain and according to the species or flora or any other rational classification the state of the soul follows the same angle of ascension which, in the mystic square, as here in the mystic circle, designates the approach to the Light of the World and Soul. Thus mathematics serves soul, while soul follows an unerring principle of geometry.

You see only what you perceive, in both a material and spiritual sense. The key to seeing is also the key to perceiving. The higher the rate of vibrations which you can command the greater will be your spiritual light. Intense rays of light, as the red, are not as potent as the more electrical, the blue, purple and indigo. The finer colors are significant of the finer vibrations, the coarser of the crude. Thus the grade of one's consciousness, which is the light of the soul, is determined by one's spirituality. The finer and purer the life the closer affinitized one is with the thought spheres of angels. Spirits and angels live and move and have their being in these spheres, that are as fixed as the unchanging law. These spheres represent as they illustrate mathematical numbers and uniform ratios of vibrations. The ratio of absolute positive vibrations is as the absolute positive sphere of harmony. It is the sphere of the apotheosis. The absolute negative sphere is its antithesis, symbol of night, darkness, death. The two harmonize at a center of polarity, which is the center of radiation.

In all planes and spheres, the light and darkness alternate by the sacred sign of Libra, the scales or balance. Libra rules the heart, spiritually, rules in love. Interlinear rays of light form the spectrum of the soul's life and Divinity where it attains access to the holy flame of love, white and pure within the Holy of Holies. By traveling to the East from the West, to the Light from Darkness, to Spirituality from Materiality, to consciousness from birth and rebirth in matter, you make the straight line, symbol of Divinity, of one, of eternity, harmony, God. At every point of the circle of spiritual light, as it blends with the circle of material light, the unchanging law reigns, and through the angles of relation to light the soul attains its state of Divinity and enters the aureole of its own mystic light of love. But the path is one of love unto love, by the process designated spirituality.

SIXTH EXPERIMENT

Write inspirationally what the spirit gives you on the theme "Light and Spirituality." To prepare conditions for this experiment become very quiet and passive and then concentrate by aspiration upon Divinity. As you receive the light of inspiration perceive the thought which is imminent. Be not baffled by failure but insist upon the success of it by patient, persistent and conscientious effort.

CLAIRVOYANCE

PART II

LESSON VII

Spirit in Relation to Time and Space. The Sphere and Office of Matter

There is no question but that there is a profound philosophy underlying the speculations of the scientist and metaphysician concerning time and space. We know that these two words, though much abused, hold in them the apparent limit of consciousness. Terminology is not to be received as nor construed to be the formula or statement of consciousness. Literature, like mathematics, has an esoteric as well as an exoteric signification; but words are the vehicles of thought, the clothing of ideas, which no more define thought in its spirituality than a suit of clothes defines man. There is a remote relation between them, but as a shadow cannot define the light which makes it, neither should words be taken as absolute interpretations of the thoughts which they clothe. Words must be given a spiritual as well as a material definition. More than this, words must be given the exact meaning which the mind that uses them wishes to have conveyed, and as there is in this respect a general and particular use, both in the material and spiritual sense, caution should be taken lest the one meaning be confused with the other or lest ambiguity be accepted for perspicuity. The real masters of form see to it that spirit defines the form, not that the form defines the spirit. This, indeed, is perfect art. Thus the words, time and space, have suffered because of a multiform definition, yet they are conspicuous in philosophy as words, that convey a different meaning to different minds. When, for instance, you literalize time and space, you make them coextensive with matter, and as matter is coextensive with spirit, both give to the words what is implied in the quality of both.

CLAIRVOYANCE

Matter is supposed to have three dimensions, length, breadth and thickness, while spirit is limited by finality or finiteness, words which signify an end to time and space. The confusion at once arises when an attempt is made to use the formula as here set forth. It is then allowed that time and space are illimitable. Yet all this is irreconcilable with the words as materially interpreted. Time is a definite concept, as the Greek word (temno) illustrates, while space is no less concrete. Yet when applied to matter, they seem to fix the plane of its action, and yet when applied to spirit, they seem to convey an entirely different impression. The cause of this we shall here attempt to explain.

Spirit is fated in spheres of action. These spheres operate in corresponding planes, which are designated by the word matter. Matter as the composition or chemical base of these planes is spirit in a crude form. All elements, as we have elsewhere taught, are spiritual in their affinities, that is, they are repelled by and attracted to psychic polarities or centers. They have no absolute existence. They have no being per se or outside of spirit. They are in fine and in crude one and the same spirit. Spirit possesses them and they manifest in the material plane through the spectrum or medium of consciousness, not as an entity or a composition of entities, but as the veritable form of the spirit, spirit having in itself the unit or primate of the kaleidoscope of these elements. Thus whatever may compose the elements or organism of the body as the unchanging law controls the forms which appear in a sphere and plane of uniform vibration. Matter in reality is but a mode of motion, fixed by the unchanging law of spirit. This is why all elements have their uniform attractions and repulsions, as well as their analogous polarities. This is also why you will find on all suns and in their systems the polarity which regulates the centrifugal and centripetal forces, and makes it but an axis on which revolve the orbs and motions of the galaxies.

CLAIRVOYANCE

The polarity itself is fixed by the unchanging law. Thus in a plane or sphere of spirit, say number one (1), a certain grade of vibrations obtains, and in them spirit operates accordingly, displaying its phenomena and revealing its expression, all the alleged elements that play in its mystic kaleidoscope conforming to the polarity of spirit, which centers its axis on uniform polarities in similars. By similars we mean modes of motion which foreshadow in a uniform ratio of development an analogous form of motion, but under a higher rate of vibration. Thus hydrogen, oxygen, argon, each and all have their ultimates in spirit. They are prototypes of a type absolute. Thus matter seems to be and is fated in conditions of time and space, both having to do with modes of the motion of spirit. The mystic circle of time and space has been likened to a circle containing 360 degrees, the degrees in space and in time corresponding exactly, the vibration in any sphere or analogous plane covering the circle in space in uniform time. In other and plain words, it takes so long to go so far in this circle of 360 degrees. One rate of vibration may be slower or more rapid than another, but the polarity of the lower is conditioned by that of the higher and acts in perfect rhythm with it. Over, beneath and through all these spheres and corresponding planes of vibration one unchanging law rules. Thus time and space are relative terms and must be so interpreted, and they must not be made the formula of the soul or the Cosmos. Time and space are words that refer to spheres and planes of psychic action and hence to modes of the soul's life or being. Chiefly they have to do with materiality and are not recognized in the calendar of spirit. Thought and action expressed in spirituality govern all concepts of eternity and show their spiritual signification in the higher life.

No time or space is there in the material sense, location or residence being subordinated to the law that acts reversely from its action in materiality. That is, whereas here the spirit is subordinated to the natural, in our realm, the natural is

CLAIRVOYANCE

subordinated to the spiritual law. The difference is one of correspondence but not one of opposition. Thus time and space are not literalized but spiritualized, the real concept of them becoming realized.

The office or sphere of matter is to bring the soul through these multiplied changes, all fixed by the unchanging law, through a uniform process of evolution into the aim of the involution, which is the apotheosis. We are not concerned with final causes, but with the mission of the facts of life, which are the collaterals of truth, the exponent of the law of being. We are not concerned with the reason but the cause for all this arrangement and from our point of view it is evident that matter serves soul in its evolution. It is a basic mode of manifestation and expression and by its own rates of vibration serves the soul in its various and uniform states of consciousness. It is in our realm as it is in the realm of coarser matter. However, the end is outworked as the spheres and planes are ever maintained in one perfect correlation and integrity. Spirit is only subordinate to this or that mode, when a state of soul reaches its perfection through it. Never can number one (1) grade of matter hold a soul that lives and moves and has its being in number two (2) grade. And so on through the mathematical series in the rhyming and mystic scale of being. Strive then for the purity of spheres where soul responds to finer grades of motion in matter and the brain will become the lens as the mind the spectrum through which the light of lights will stream and bring its own wondrous kaleidoscope.

SEVENTH EXPERIMENT

Do you sense a slow or rapid vibration by holding this name in your hand? In attempting this experiment place the name written in ink on your brow or in the palm of the left hand and note the sensation. If the person is intense, impulsive, magnetic or electrical, or the reverse, the result will be very apparent. Keen concentration and unruffled receptivity of mind lead to immediate and the best results. The same experiment may apply to superscriptions of letters or any articles suffused with personal magnetism.

CLAIRVOYANCE

LESSON VIII

Spirit in Relation to Control. The Uses of Magnetism and Electricity. Hypnotism. The Trance

Control in spiritual science should not be confused with control or "controls" as popularized by spiritualism. Control, as we use it, has to do with the will and not with the organism; it is never forced and it refers to choice on the part of the spirit who wishes to avail himself of its benefits. The word control has been very much abused, as much to the detriment of spiritualism as a factor for enlightenment and civilization as to the detriment of those who submitted to it. Among the media, it is the usurpation of the will of another, a dominance of one mind over another for malevolent or benevolent purposes. It is, in short, obsession and not possession. To be self or soul possessed is not to be obsessed. Many, therefore, are obsessed who, could they understand the law of mediumship or control, would not so readily accede to control. We are not here arguing against or criticizing a mode or the method of excarnate spirit communication. We hold that obsession as control has its needs and uses, but we are inclined to believe that were the dangers of control, as illustrated by obsession, perceived or understood, few indeed would open their will to its power. There are spirits who, not yet having arisen above the attractions of earth, and who, entangled in its magnetic waves of influence, seek through mediumship an avenue of approach to the old and familiar scenes and haunts of pleasure and vice; and thus precious years are seemingly wasted by these spirits in thus seeking to live over or relive the old scenes while the impulse from within the soul for higher individualistic work is temporarily baffled. These unfortunate ones, blinded by their attractions, like ducks that mistake decoys for their own kind, rush into organisms and seek to continue the earth life or find in the sea of materiality, whither the earth attractions draw them, the means to psychic gratification or expiation; whereas, it is literally true that such license on the part of spirit and medium are weapons of offense rather than defense. It is not to be denied that some good is achieved by these spirits, directly and indirectly, nor is it at all to be wondered at that such intervention should be hailed by earth dwellers as a boon; but while this is so and while it follows, yet who would deny that the better course is to be set at naught for it? Who would say that spirit by obsession acquires what can only be received by receptivity to angel ministrations? It is as if the spirit of an adult should by hypnotism usurp and obsess the will and body of an infant, the better by so doing to correct mistakes made or gather up lessons omitted in the sphere of infancy. The law is that we shall unfold progressively, not retrogressively, by pushing on and into higher and diviner states of consciousness, not by reacting the scenes of one sphere and plane of existence, or by receiving the lessons which are no longer needful. We have this obstacle to remove from the thought of many who enter spirit life unprepared, so to speak, for the encampment on the hillsides of summer land, who, ignorant of psychic law and its attractions, mistake earth loves for the law and thus swim out on those magnetic seas that influx the celestial and terrestrial planes and seek to renew life in the body. Experience in the spirit world has taught us that control and its law have a deeper and diviner import than that which is illustrated by commonplace obsession. We affirm that, while obsession is permitted and is necessary as an alternative, while beneficent results follow invasions of spirits of the old haunts of earth, while medium/ship which has opened the door for intercommunication of spirits and mortals has served and now serves an admirable and commendable purpose; yet, while all this is true, the law of control serves soul to higher and diviner ends. The original intent of spirits who passed out of the body in returning to earth and earth loves was to live in the atmosphere of their natural attractions, and it became at once the mission as well as arduous task of the more advanced spirits, under the ministrations of angels, to teach them the necessity of withdrawing from earth and winging their flight to more celestial environments. Nay, more than this, it was the aim of missionary spirits to posit themselves as a rescue band or a soul-saving crew at the portal of each one's home, and as death cut asunder the silvery thread which associates and binds the spirit with and to the body, there to apply the science of control. Naturally, the spirit, freed of the entanglement of earth, seeks at once the visions celestial and curiosity prompts it to peer into the corridors of heaven and seek for entrance to the more celestial spheres, and upon being denied access to them, and finding that earth loves are more potent than psychic attractions of the celestial order, it, by the very necessity of its life, recedes from the light of spirit, and, for a while at least, entertains the desire to be once again with the loved ones of earth. The potency of this love, which is an intense attraction, lures it earthward, and down the pathway of earth attractions it descends until once more it identifies itself with the circle of earth. Its pursuit is for the gateway of mediumship that leads to actuality of earth attractions and consciousness, and as such pursuit is a very difficult and weary one, and fraught with untold disappointments, sorrows and dangers, a spirit in search of this golden fleece, like Jason of Greek mythology, can come to but one conclusion and one end.

And so it is. The gateway found and opened, the spirit is for years kept in the atmosphere of earth, without the sweet consolation of superior souls who shed their glory upon it, chilled by the cold atmosphere of earth or only warmed when a familiar face smiles upon it or a word or message is exchanged at the curtain of a cabinet or through the diversified channels of mediumship. Years are spent in such action, which may well be likened to if not called an adventure. The question at once arises, could not this same communication be effected after the manner of science rather than ignorance, after the manner of those guardian spirits who have learned the law of control and seek to teach it without money and price to all the newly born into the spirit world; and, if so, should not spirits who now roam the earth, seeking to obsess as well as obsessing mortals, be benefited thereby? Would not mortals learn a lesson by the discovery and teaching?

The law of control has then a material and spiritual phase and signification, the latter ruling and dictating the sphere of the former. Thus, to rightly control mind, you really control organism, as when the will is directed by the purpose of the unchanging law, the appetites, passions and desires bend to the decree of the will. To obsess or control organism, as is illustrated in spiritualism, is to operate the law materially, but to guide the mind by operating the spirituality of control, that is, by fulfilling the real purpose of the law, is not to dispossess any mortal or spirit of its body or its prerogative by usurping its sphere and plane of being. The real signification of control is inspiration, teaching, guidance, not usurpation or obsession, and while obsession in the sphere of control may be said to be and is fundamental to the end of control, control as we would have you apply it is spiritual rather than material. Ample provision is made in the desideratum of Nature's law for so-called "lost opportunities." And as there are and can be no lost opportunities, each sphere and plane of life serving the soul exactly in mathematical order, there is no need of spirits returning to earth to be re-embodied by means of control, or to seek through mediumship to live again through another's organism what it enjoyed or failed to enjoy. A dire and baleful effect is produced upon humanity by so doing.

The object of mediumship, as we perceive it, is for real action, to make the ignorant aware of the eternal consciousness of spirit and to nourish and replenish the earth and its denizens with the light of the skies, but when such purpose is perverted or ignored, and when mediumship affords spirits the means for the untold sins of life, spirits becoming like mistletoes or barnacles, sapping the vital forces from the mediums for self-gratification, as is often the case, our teaching and the value of it will at once be perceived. Therefore we urge the higher spiritual aspect and spiritualizing uses of control. Control, then, is the law by which spirits in or out of the body affect through the will by hypnotism, or the use of electricity and magnetism, an identity of action, psychic, mental and organic, with their own. It has two special forms, as it has, as we have elsewhere stated, two particular phases. Its phases are material and spiritual, that of inspiration, as in mental illumination of seers and the inspired media, and that of the trance, where the spirit of the medium is set at naught by hypnotism. Its forms are dependent and independent. The dependent is the automatic, where the consciousness of the medium is displaced or in a sense merged into, if not absorbed by the consciousness of, the controlling intelligence. The trance is the dependent or automatic phase and form. The inspirational is the independent form and phase. To induce the automatic form of control a preponderance of magnetism is used, and you will find that all magnetists or hypnotists are batteries for this force.

To induce the independent or inspirational form of control, electricity is used, that is, in preponderance, and you will find that all inspired media or seers speak and see with their eyes open and are conscious of what is said through them. Not only is this true, but the law holds good throughout the sphere and plane of mediumship. All mediums for physical or material forms of the spiritual manifestations are batteries for the magnetic force, that is, they supply an organism sufficiently negatived by electricity and positived by magnetism to establish a polarity for the use of the latter, which is the condition of matter as electricity is the condition of spirit. All mediums for mental forms of the spiritual manifestations are batteries for the electrical force, that is, they supply an organism that is sufficiently negatived by magnetism and positived by electricity to establish a polarity for the use of the latter, which is the condition of spirit, as the former is the condition of matter. Thus you have the phenomena of the medium, through magnetism and electricity, of the material and spiritual form. All mediums are both magnetic and electrical, the physical having a preponderance of the former, while the mental having the preponderance of the latter. It will at once be seen that the automatic phase, both among the physical and mental media, is induced largely through the use of magnetism, while the independent, that of inspiration, or illumination, is induced by the use of electricity. Automatic writers are those whose beings are harmoniously polarized by the magnetic and electrical forces; so with trance speakers. Those who have produced through their organism both inspiration and the material phenomena, each class successful in their phase, are mediums whose organism responds as readily to the magnetic as to the electrical vibrations, and could be put into the trance, if the operating spirit intelligences so desired. Such represent the shoots of the new order of mediums; they are the illustrations of the Nemesis of the new dispensation of spiritualism.

Hypnotism and the trance are cause and effect; that is, one leads to the other through the potency of the will. Concentration is the key that solves the mystery. Hypnotism is the power of all because it is the prerogative of spirit. The mother that soothes the babe into sleep on her bosom is obeying the law that closes at night the Eyes of the World. And creation is as surely hypnotized, when at the hour appointed for the earth to recede into darkness, although it is unconscious of the process and to the manner born, as when an expert hypnotist induces it by artificial or psychic means. The trance is a form of sleep. Sleep is the only natural trance that is known; all other forms, either the automatic or independent in mediumship, are higher forms of consciousness. Sleep proves but never disproves consciousness as by dreams, and the trance reveals its own

CLAIRVOYANCE

absence of consciousness. There cannot be dreams or knowledge where consciousness is not. The highest form of trance in mediumship is the one where consciousness is most aware of the interior illumination; such is the apotheosis of trance. It is the perfection of control because the perfection of possession. It is the state of soul where the will of the Divine in the will of another is most fully and clearly perceived and realized. It is conformity to the Law of Uniformity in all. It is the culmination and illustration of the deific principle illustrated by the seer of Nazareth, "I am in the Father and the Father in me, the work that I do I do not of myself." It is cooperative and reciprocal and becomes the spectrum of the will of God. This can be attained, not by obsession, not by control, as is illustrated in the sphere and phenomena of catalepsy, but by the atonement of the spirit with the Spirit of the Universe. To unfold this form of control you must seek for and know the law that gives it, and first of all you must, by spirituality, intensify your zeal and love for truth, that having access to knowledge you may use it wisely and well, that having mediumship you may become one with the Divine Unity of the Cosmos, that revealing and having revealed the spiritual manifestations, you may become ennobled and blessed thereby.

EIGHTH EXPERIMENT

Climb in thought to the highest sphere within your soul and perceive how this law operates. Note the results of this experiment. Enter into the silence of spirit.

LESSON IX

COLOR: ITS DEFINITION AND MEANING

There is and can be no more interesting study of Nature and in Nature than that of color. The law of color lies at the foundation of psychic attractions and permeates the life. Whatever material science may teach concerning color adds to the interest already aroused on the subject. Color itself seems to be the atmosphere of all things, and as such, holds in its force the chemistry of its operations and manifestations. It is not the atmosphere of anything, however, but so wholly or completely does it transfuse both essence and form, that, like the atmosphere, it seems to be the medium of life itself. Color is not an entity. Both light and sound are motions, induced by thought, being the vibrations of thought in harmonial spheres and planes of attraction. And color, like both light and sound, is a quality or degree of motion. We teach that color in the absolute sense does not exist, as pure thought and pure motion is colorless. Color suggests an agent and medium of communication. Between black and white in the relative and absolute form there is no radical difference. The distinction is in the circle of materiality and spirituality. In form, as in essence, color bears and interprets a reciprocal relation. Black in materiality refers to black in spirituality, and in the soul or in psychic attractions lie the exponent of one color and all colors. Pure thought, or thought perfect, is colorless, as is likewise that thought which generates black in materiality and spirituality. Every impure or black thought has its "mate" in spirit and its correspondence. Thoughts, as personalities or souls, pass through the same mode of development from black to white, from effect to cause, from birth in matter to the apotheosis or Divinity. But do not understand us as teaching that thoughts are either entities or the form of entities as things. Thoughts are the substance of the soul

CLAIRVOYANCE

as matter may be likened to the substance of spirit or drops of water may be likened to the substance of the ocean, without which the ocean could have no meaning.

Thought, in spheres of expression, reveals the soul's approach or ascent to Divinity, it designates the degree of attainment in the circle of the grand man. Thoughts illustrate soul in spheres and planes of expression and manifestation and by color reveal the sphere. Thus, with the three primary colors, derived from the one perfect motion, blending by polarity into the black and white, the negative and the positive form, the red, the blue and the yellow, you have the four complimentary colors or the seven derivatives. The octave is one in seven, one in two, and three in four, through a series of one, two, three, four and seven expressions. Thus, with the pure white as the basis of Divinity, and black as its manifestation, you have the unfoldment of red, the blood, illustrating the heart and love, and blue, illustrating the brain or wisdom, and the yellow, illustrating the light of the spirit which is evolved through the psychic ray from within in marriage with the solar ray from without. The yellow is regarded as the result of the white, both materially and spiritually, polarized by an equal ratio of red and blue. And all the intermediary hues are shades of white in parts of blue and red, under the influence of the ray of light from without. Yellow itself is a form of white under the vibration of red, but blue and red have a more occult inclination and analysis. The blue and the red refer to the spirit embodied and polarized in matter; and as such they illustrate electrical and magnetic forces in equal parts, one (i) shade of blue corresponds to one (i) shade of red in results of yellow in aspect to white, and ever is this scale the formula of interpretation, because color obeys, as it illustrates and embodies, the law of rhythm. White is the solvent and basis of all electrical and magnetic combinations. Black is negative and stands in occultism for matter or materiality, and in spiritual science for ignorance, evil, earthliness, the alleged sinister forces and crude elements of Nature. White is positive, and in occultism stands for spirit or spirituality, and in spiritual science for wisdom, good, heavenliness. Thus the light of day is in eternal contrast to the night, and forces of the one, which are electrical, ever act in maximum power against and with the magnetic forces of darkness or night. Electricity is positive while magnetism is negative in the problem of the soul, immured in matter. Thus the soul or spirit is ever positive to matter and the astral vibrations, and has in it the law of sovereignty. Matter is ever negative to spirit, as black is to white or night is to day. At a time in the solar year in the calendar of earth when the ratio between day and night, between the electrical and magnetic forces, is fixed by a perfect polarity, these seemingly antagonistic forces play in perfect unity. Then is the hour for spirit communion and receptivity. At all other times, in concentration and centralization, the psyche must exercise a more potent will force to set at naught the outward electrical vibrations in aspect to the spirit's negativeness, against which it operates. This is not for a malefic end or purpose, but to serve psyche or soul.

If we should teach that all color reveals the polarity of these two forces in aspect to soul, we shall, as we believe, state what is actually true. Spirit establishes by the inherent law of affinity the spherical polarity between electrical and magnetic vibrations, which, as we have taught, designate the white and black, the positive and negative forms of psyche in expression and manifestation. Thus, as electricity and magnetism are modes of motion, fixed by the unchanging Law within the soul, they, through the operation of spirit, give the kaleidoscope of colors, which are so beautiful to sense or behold. And as in number one (1) sphere and plane, the white of the spirit, in yellow expresses itself through red and blue, the psychic lenses or spectrum of mind and body, you have the chemistry of all colors, the seven and three, the two and one, in the myriad of interblendings. Each shade expresses a thought as each thought is an Interpretation of psyche. Thus, at the center of mind and heart, through the white in blue and the white in red, you have a result in yellow, and the spirit, as well as its aura, shines in the colors of its own expression. Nay, more than this, could the chemistry of material colors be penetrated or known, it would be found, not only that each shade corresponds to a degree in the ray of white or the mystic circle of psyche, that each color, whatever may be its form or wherever it may be found, illustrates a certain number of mathematical vibrations, exact and uniform in harmonial and reciprocal spheres and planes of expression and manifestation, but that at the center of heart, which is ruled through the mind, and at the center of the mind, which is ruled through the heart, love, the Divine Principle of Psyche, establishes the absolute polarity. So that all color finds its basis and interpretation in this absolute polarity.

Affinity is the law by which this polarity is maintained in all the spheres. You are, by this polarity, reaching the apotheosis in love; and each sphere, radiating a color, fixed by this polarity, in the earth or in any other planet, marks the psychic unfoldment. At once it can be seen that if any shade of red, blue or yellow, black or white, purple or green, be your hue, you are allied by electrical and magnetic polarization with all forms that radiate them. So that you have your correspondence in minerals, in the flora, in the fauna of the Cosmos. You have, in short, your psychic attractions, so far as color is concerned, to fire, earth, water, air, for was it not said by the Pythagoreans and mystics of Egypt and Asia that earth is red, water blue, fire white and air yellow, and in them is not the soul prefigured and foreshadowed?

And thus, the ascent of psyche by spirituality is made. The white light of love, operating on mind and heart, in a positive and negative polarity of the red and blue of the forces of magnetism and electricity, evoking by a myriad of combinations of color, the angel of the skies. And ever from black, the night of

CLAIRVOYANCE

birth, psyche, rises in the lap of earth, which is the red, and above the blue, the water, by the sun, the yellow, until by death and regeneration the veil of matter is destroyed and the veil of spirituality, analogous in color is given, fire, not water, white, at last purifying psyche from all black; love, conquering evil, her negative, through the potency of the Divine.

NINTH EXPERIMENT

Read clairvoyantly the color of anyone's mental and spiritual aura. What color does the spirituality make? In making this experiment attention should be given to color waves which pass before the clairvoyant vision. Sometimes the vision of these color waves is sensed, rather than perceived, and is shown in symbols which must be interpreted.

Note that coarse colors give disagreeable sensations, while fine and delicate tints impress one happily.

CLAIRVOYANCE

LESSON X

Clairvoyance and Consciousness in Relation to Spiritual Perception

That clairvoyance and consciousness have a relation to the spiritual perception is the evident fact of this series of Teachings. Whatever may be the illumination or penetration of clairvoyance, and whatever may be the state or unfoldment of consciousness that the spiritual perceptions use and foreshadow, the spiritual perception is the "reason" of intuition, and by reason we do not refer to cause or source but to law. As the mind has reason, so the spirit in the interior operations, as intuition, has reason. In other words, reason is to mind what the spiritual perception is to intuition. Intuition and tuition refer to spheres of knowledge, the latter to knowledge acquired through the senses and the former acquired through divine inspiration. Intuition and tuition have to do with consciousness in the sphere of clairvoyance, but reason is the law of tuition as perception is the law of intuition. The law is one and unchanging in both forms of consciousness. In psychology, reason is closely affinitized to intuition, and so is it, and so should it be, in all spheres of consciousness. Reason may well be called the exterior or posterior guide of spirit, for it is by reason that spirit unfolds. Intuition is higher in its sphere; it has to do with consciousness in the enfolded, unfolding- and unfolded states; it is ever adjudged by reason before it is made the mode or rule of action, occult as the decision may be, yet it is focused through reason and reaches the mind or outward consciousness in this wise. You may walk by reason in both the outward and inward sense, but never do you walk by either one alone. Always do they interact, and when they harmoniously interact in a perfect polarity, then there is perfect spiritual development.

CLAIRVOYANCE

The spiritual perception as the "reason" of intuition has to do with clairvoyance and consciousness, not in the outward but the inward sense. In the mind and all that relates consciousness to it, reason is regnant, and it is through reason that both tuition and intuition are extended. As long as reason balks the way to progress and unfoldment in the interior sense, it no longer waits upon intuition and has become habituated to one mode of action or thought; in other words, it seeks for conformity in uniformity by conforming variety to a segregated form of unity. One word will explain reason in this aspect, and it is prejudice. Prejudice is reason subsidized. Reason should in the natural and spiritual sense be free to act according to evidence or facts. But where it is conformist in its action, it is disarmed of its power and prerogative and is a terrible engine for evil. Where reason is open to or receptive of divine inspiration and acts harmoniously with conscience and perception in the light of both tuition and intuition, you have a sphere of consciousness, beautiful to behold and more beautiful to realize. It has been said that reason is a more potent guide to knowledge than perception, and vice versa; but neither statement is wholly true. Each can and does guide, but together they are absolute. One may be guided by reason, witness the scientist and experimentalist, or by perception, witness the religionist and metaphysician, or by both, witness the philosopher and seer; and in each case excellent and beneficent results are attained. But the absolute test of power and being is in the latter case, where, as is illustrated by the seer, the field of vision and action becomes the whole sphere of consciousness, where reason through perception, and perception through reason, is utilized, and humanity thus attains the ideal or spiritual; not by subverting the practical but by unfolding life by the Law of Soul. Thus, both clairvoyance and consciousness should wait upon both reason and perception in this twofold sense, and for reasons which we shall now specify.

CLAIRVOYANCE

Firstly, that a line of demarcation should be drawn between that which belongs to the sphere of mind in the realm of tuition and that which belongs to the mind in the realm of intuition. Secondly, that you may discern that which is the natural seeing and natural perceiving, and that which is spiritual seeing and spiritual perceiving. Thirdly, that you may know that which is from intuition and tuition in the sphere of telepathy and divine inspiration. Fourthly, that you may discern impressions, clairvoyantly received, through the action of the perception on finer ethers in concentration on spirit and spiritual things, and that which is the actual impression of an operating spirit intelligence.

Thus, by such analysis, you will have acquired a facility for scientific methods and spiritual penetration far beyond your most ardent dreams, and besides, you will have attained the rapport of seers, seeing and perceiving in the sphere of clairvoyance and consciousness whether in the body or out of it.

EXPERIMENT X

As a test we offer this experiment: Make comparisons of the specifications here enumerated and observe the sources and methods of reason and perception.

CLAIRVOYANCE

LESSON XI

How Man is Unfolded in Inspiration, Clairvoyance and Psychometry: The Spirits' Laboratory

This theme is the most interesting as well as the most fascinating in the entire program of Teachings. First, because it reveals the *modus operandi* of spirit; and, secondly, because the law of mediumship is made practical and operative.

The mystery of the law of medial unfoldment is in the fact that spirit is not understood. Were spirit and its nature known, the law of its manifestation and expression would not be involved in mystery; rather, all of its processes would be both open and simple. Viewing Nature from our plane of vision and operation, the spirit presents a most varied spectacle. It is as if Nature were a vast loom, in which the warp and woof were the life forces, an, through and in which psyche, the soul, by threads of light, so delicate and extenuated that no spectrum of earth could reveal them, weaves the manifestation of form. And so exact is the form as a representation of the idea of the essence or psyche, that, unless counteracting agencies mar the perfection of it, it is a copy of the psyche, so far as matter is able to plagiarize spirit or the ideas of spirit.

This, however, is most beautifully accomplished in the loom of Nature. Few flaws in her handiwork can be found. The chalice of the lily or rose is more often immaculate in conception and of spotless purity than otherwise. The planets and galaxies, as well as the tiniest atom, illustrate the Divinity of Nature and the superiority of her power. No thread fails to carry out the original purpose of the master mind. From the cloister of the spirit where the white light of spirit burns in pristine purity to the shell where it glows in the form of matter, the integrity of the design is intact, and therefore faultless. Could you perceive this by observing Nature in her own laboratory or workshop, you would form an idea or derive a plan of the operation of the spirit in the development of medial powers in sensitives and mediums. Nature is capable of developing the sensitive by an invariable law, which, though slow in its action, is sure in its results; but spirit excarnate can assist Nature, that is, while neither increasing nor decreasing her balance of power, it can arrange conditions for her results. Let it not be forgotten that the science of medial unfoldment is not contrary to but in harmony with Nature's law, and that it affords spirits the key to the end which she foreshadows. Thus, when a sensitive, by Nature's law, through experience and education, is ready for the office of mediumship, to blossom forth into the practical work of a medium, and thus discharge the duty which such an one may owe to Divinity, the spirit world arranges the necessary conditions for such an one's birth and work. The kindred souls, those that are afifinitized to the person, and who have been, by a wise Providence, held within the sphere of such an one's attractions, feel and see the hour of deliverance approaching, and great care is taken that such an one receives the best and finest thought waves and ethereal forces for the new birth or phase of work. The immediate time is the most serious and important, for then is it the duty of wise spirits on the immortal side of life to see to it that the physical frame or organism is adapted to the changes which are being inwrought. It is as if the person were being readjusted.

Yet readjustment, in this respect, is not to be confused with Nature's purpose and law; for whatever may be the end or object of mediumship, Nature invariably amplifies and perfects it through her causation. What we mean by readjustment of the organism is the adaptation of the outward form to the work of the spirit excarnate, that as in the true and natural sense and sphere organism reflects what is within and external to spirit, yet it serves the spirit through matter rather than through the spiritual body. The outward or material form answers the needs of the spirit in its expression, and this is why the spirit is "naturalized."

The whole establishment of the senses and faculties, comprehended by human nature, is called into existence through the embodiment of psyche. Out of the plane of matter psyche needs no material form, and no apparatus for reaching a material form, such as the nervous system or the sense system, but inasmuch as the sense realm is the reflex of the psychic realm, and could have no existence and manifestation were it not for their correspondences or correspondence in psyche, the need of them becomes at once apparent. The order in the spiritual world is the reverse of the order in the natural world; that is, spirit incarnate acts outwardly and inwardly through materiality and a polarity established through the ratio of forces in their geometrical and increased expression toward matter, while spirit excarnate in its operation upon matter reaches the sense plane inversely or reversely, as has been declared, through another but corresponding polarity. In the normal man the brain and mind are polarized to balance the subtler and finer psychic forces of the spirit. But in the readjustment the medium's organism is depolarized materially, so as to be capable of reflecting all that is possible with the excarnate spirit under its established polarity.

This polarization of both planes is only possible with mediums where the natural sensitiveness of the organism responds to either order of vibrations and where no injury can be done. Nature acts normally in both realms, affording all that is needful to the perfection of the expression of the medium, so far as materiality is concerned, and affording, also, all that is needful to the perfection of the excarnate spirit in the uses to which it puts mediumship. The organism and spirit of the medium are so adjusted to the spiritual body and spirit of the controlling or affinitizing spirit or spirits that its thought need but be reflected in the spirit of the medium, when the control is affected by the will of the spirit, to be vibrated through the harmonial planes and spheres of psychic, mental and organic spectra, and received in the form that the guide wished. Sensitiveness is a state of mental receptivity as well as organic readjustment to psychic planes of impressibility. The organism, being subject to the law of matter in the natural world, and the law of spirit in the spiritual world, is thus interacted upon, and the most perfect concentration of mind is necessary, where the organism is not responsive to the will of the excarnate intelligence, or even where it is in perfect accord, so that no mar or jar may occur in the translation of the idea. Very few, indeed, even of the media, understand the delicacy of the relation, and thus errors are transmitted to the material plane and form a large percentage of the pabulum sent to hungry mortals by the spirit world, which, were the concentration perfect, both as to receptivity and impressibility of all concerned, could altogether be avoided. Mediumship is but another name for the ability of an embodied spirit or mortal to reflect through a polarization of spirit in reverse relation to its normal life, by a perfect affinitization of organism, so far as its impressibility is concerned, and with spirit, so far as its receptivity is concerned, that which is given from the operating, excarnate spirit intelligence.

Mediumship enables an excarnate spirit to reverse the normal order of spirit in the form and apply the process of action that obtains on the ethereal plane. Yet, in all the diversified forms of mediumship, the work of the excarnate spirit is affected by a conformity to material laws, conditions and elements. Psychic force is used instead of instrumentalities. The medium is thus organized and prepared for his work and it is easily seen that the degree of the work done or to be done by the spirit world depends entirely upon the absoluteness of the control or guidance. Where there is disharmony or pride, selfishness or vice to contend with, not only will the manifestations be impaired and distorted, if not dispersed, but the development will be retarded and violent. There is a divine signification to mediumship. It obeys a law of soul. It follows a force as eternal and immutable as God. So let it be received.

The descent of this light from the higher spheres is a wonderful event to the spirit world, and it means much for the truth. In the spirit, where this birth or development is at first seen, the process and travail are so delicate and refined that it is seldom noticed or felt ; but when the light reaches and hence operates on the form, in the transfusion and depolarization of the particles of matter, and when the repolarization, in the spiritual sense, of the nerve centers takes place inversely to their normal action, as when the birth throes are on the physical form, then there is more or less pain. Then is it that the mediumship is reaching its normal and dual action.

To effect this development is to let Nature take her course. All development must be outwrought by Nature's formula. Galvanic and hypnotic forces may effect an apparent growth, but the process of incubation in spiritualism is not the real means to the real end. Hypnotism is a dangerous expedient. Mediumship is spiritual in its sphere, inception and office and can be reached and unfolded best by Nature's invariable formula. Thus, when the spirit world, that is ever alert for the chosen ones, behold any who are about to blossom into medial unfoldment, certain guides, divinely appointed for their work and qualified for their sphere of inspiration, select out of other affinitized spirits those who are consecrated to the office of mediumship and who, by the elements which they are able to give to the medium by means of an inter-psychic harmony, afford a sure and permanent basis of action. Where this guidance is not effected, a medium is subject, by a variable polarity of attractions and repulsions, to all kinds of influences, in and out of the body, but where harmony of spirit and organism reigns,

CLAIRVOYANCE

where the normal equilibrium of spirituality, through the power of self control, is attained, there is perfect action in the law and results of the law of mediumship. The medium's brain as a terrestrial magnet, is polarized by the magnet or battery of the finer spirit forces, ethereal in their nature; the spirits in concentration acting uniformly in thought, which responds spiritually to the poles of the medium's brain and the poles of the spirit's external batteries at a center of radiation. And thus, through this means, the phenomena, in the material and mental realm, are produced. To affect this polarity is the object of spirits in development; and when the physical vibrations in the action of the organism correspond to the mental vibrations in the action of the brain, and all harmonize with the action of the spirits in the concentration of their forces and batteries, then a medium is ready for work. There is this to be said concerning the law that relates spirits to the media as guides or messengers. There is no selection, as is commonly anticipated or understood among mortals, unless the selection be understood to be the pre-ordained arrangements of Nature. Guides, like atoms, have their attractions. They stand for and embody certain principles, and are as much within the influence of a medium to whom they are attracted as the gas designated oxygen is within the ethers of earth. There is cause and reason for all attractions.

Each soul has its natural polarity in the attractions and repulsions of souls; all are not drawn into the same soul sphere nor to the same plane of revealment and manifestation of thought. And as each soul finds its own in the negative and positive relation, so each medium in the psychic sphere obeys the law which ensphers its beloved angels. And as is the degree of the circle of the expression and the collateral environments, so the psychic attractions. All great souls, on the excarnate side of life, reach to their own through the ramified and various planes and spheres of spirit, and thus the triangle, the double triangle, or the square and the circle, illustrate how, from one point to two

CLAIRVOYANCE

and from two to one, three lines measure the square of materiality and the circle of spirituality, all souls on all planets responding to one law that draws each and all to one divine center of life, light and love.

ELEVENTH EXPERIMENT

Make a clairvoyant reading. In making this experiment, use the following formula. Note the impressions and visions which impinge upon the mind as you touch or enter into communication with the person or thing.

FORMULA

1. Describe the person or thing; the person as to character, temperament and personality; the thing as to size, nature, material.

2. Describe the past, present and future.

3. As to person: Adaptation in life, mental and business endowments. As to thing: Location, migrations, uses.

4. As to person : Travel, sickness, changes, accidents, deaths. As to thing: History.

5. As to person: Who are friends or enemies and who are apt to be friend or enemy? As to thing: Its effect on life.

6. Describe the spirits that you see in and out of the body as to appearance. State names, ages, conditions. What message is given? As to thing: What scenes and visions are evoked.

7. General remarks.

LESSON XII

THE HIGHER ASPECTS OF CLAIRVOYANCE

All gifts of the spirit may be abused, that is, not used as the unchanging law of psyche designed. They may be subsidized for purposes which are temporal and not employed for ends which are divine. We here speak of the spiritual gifts and of mediumship in contradistinction to talents or genius, or even psychometry in its restricted sense and uses; and therefore the sensitive should remember that whatever may be his phase or phases of mediumship, he will be held accountable for and the good that he attains will be perceived and determined by the consecration of these gifts to their true end. The fortuneteller, palmist, card reader, clairvoyant, are doing a work in a sense helpful to humanity and honorable, but, ignorant of the import of the science to which they owe their fortune and success, they pervert, either unknowingly or knowingly, its sacred aims, and while vitiating public opinion, at the same time undermine the foundation of faith in the genuine manifestations and inspirations of the spirit. Much more should be said upon this all-important feature of the subject than would at first seem feasible, and yet the cause of spiritualism will defend itself by its own work against the enemies outside of or within its own household.

The sensitive seeking clairvoyant development is too apt to be affected by the material uses to which clairvoyance can be put, and the practical ends to be attained thereby, than by the interior and spiritual blessings which follow a perfect consecration of one's powers to divine ends. Each one seems to be seeking for manifestations, to see something and somewhat, rather than to perceive the subjective or causal operations of the spirit and the extended range of forces and principles which make up the sphere of the soul's life and Divinity. It is not to be deplored that this is so, nor is such seeking to be deprecated, but it is strange that all should not unfold such clairvoyance in the sphere of which the light and law of the spirit could be perceived and realized. The spiritual manifestations on the objective and subjective planes have a purpose, and that purpose is in the formal way to reveal the expression and consciousness of the soul; not to hold one to a fixed kaleidoscope of material forms, simply as a thing of beauty, but to impress upon each one through them the sense of duty. Thus there is a line of demarcation to be drawn between a medium who literalizes or materializes spiritual things, and cares naught for or refuses to be led into the higher Teachings of the spirit, and one who, while recognizing the sphere of mediumship, yet consecrates all mediumship to Divinity; shows by teaching and perception that matter is the vessel into which the spirit pours its forces and light, to open up the interior psychic realms and place the mind upon heavenly things.

To be able to see clairvoyantly and give trance or independent tests of spirit presences is well in its place, but such work is altogether auxiliary to the real work and office of the spirit on both sides of life. Clairvoyance in its higher aspects is divination through a consciousness illumined and unfolded by spirituality. Spirituality without or with mediumship is the key to psychic realization. Mediumship through the mental and physical phases proves objectively the deathless consciousness and postmortem power of spirits, but spirituality here and everywhere makes this an experience and a realization. There are those who are mediums and spiritualists who are both unregenerate and material; that is, they have not yet been "born of the spirit," baptized with its own fire of inspiration. To those who, like Nicodemus, seek to understand the esoteric significance of the exoteric fact of birth, Jesus points not to the phenomena of embodiment through the generative processes of Nature, but to the awakening of the spirit as out of a sleep into a consciousness of the spirit as an immortal being. And this awakening is attained through spirituality and leads to consecration. There is no question but that the mission of modern spiritualism is to place both spirit and mediumship in a sphere where their uses and purposes will be perceived, and where mediums as well as their disciples will have no other propaganda than the inspirations of truth. When this shall have been attained, jealousy, envy, spite, selfishness among the media and workers will have ceased, and the world will reap the peaceful benefits of a spotless and consecrated representation of the forces of heaven. This is the higher aspect of clairvoyance as viewed from the standpoint of mediumship and the uses to which spiritual gifts should be put.

There is, however, an aspect to clairvoyance as a factor of consciousness which we wish now to mention, and which, if fully understood, refers to benefits to sensitives, mediums and all who are interested in their psychic development. If the exercise of mediumship in the sphere of clairvoyance has material advantages, surely there are spiritual that have not been realized. If clairvoyance enables you to see spirits in and out of the body, time and space being no barriers, surely it also enables you to perceive the height, depth and breadth of the Principle, operative and imminent in all forms of life, in life itself. And this is the all-important aspect to which we wish to call your attention, for two reasons: First, that you may be divinely human in the exercise of your conscience, will, faculties and prerogatives; secondly, that you may know your sphere and plane in the cosmos. That clairvoyance can procure you these benefits is evidenced by the facts which it affords of divination. The consciousness, symbol of the All Seeing Eye, is free to perceive the fullness of God. In it God is reflected and revealed, but the quality and intensity of the reflection and revelation depend altogether upon the grade of spirituality. As spirituality deepens and partakes more and more of the principle of the soul, it opens the sphere of spiritual light, and in that atmosphere the spirit perceives God. To perceive the object of the unchanging law is not to remove from one planet to another, nor to force the apotheosis by magic, if that could be done, but it is to look into psyche from the plane and sphere in which you manifest, and unfolding yourself into the highest degree in the circle of your expression on earth, to utilize the light that belongs to you. For the mission of spiritualism through mediumship and clairvoyance or seership is to show that you are as near to psyche here on this planet, as near to the principle of being, as near to God, as you ever can be, and that since you can really communicate with the Divine Principle of all Being through Nature and her myriads of forms and denizens of life, so you can spiritually commune with this spirit in the realm of consciousness. Forms but veil the spirit; they do not set it at naught; they but manifest it; they do not make communication impossible. The spirit when true penetrated reveals the law of its embodiments and expressions, and this clairvoyance elaborates and elucidates. It is then the privilege of all souls to penetrate the interior spirit of the universe and grow potent and divine through spirituality. This is the key to the realms on high, the happy gateway to the sky. This is the light of consciousness that men have said never was on sea or land, but is perceived behind the curtain of the senses. This is the realm where as from a universal, unchanging and eternal polarity souls swarm to catch the breath of the Light of the World. This is the heart of the White Rose, that fashions each petal white, that the eye may see the beauty of the spirit and know that art and Nature lead to love and peace.

EXPERIMENT XII

Withhold nothing, but notice how the principles of seeing and perceiving open up the circle of life eternal in all worlds. Concentrate on this principle and swim out on its vibration to the outermost and innermost Reality.

CLAIRVOYANCE

BENEDICTION

With this spirit of research you have naught to fear. The temple of wisdom and of the living God is yours to possess and enjoy. In its pure, white light that burns at its altar there is no shadow or changing. Its inspiration is perfect, its power all embracing, its love surpassingly sweet.

Within the cloister or cabinet of its walls angels meet with one accord and spirit; overarching it is unbounded love.

Nature is its oracle and her law is perfect. Thus, dear friends, make the anabasis of the soul, from the depths to the heights, out of the sense realm into the spirit of all things, that the soul may have no veil between it and God, but that Divinity and Humanity may be one in Harmony, Light, Consciousness and Peace. Go forth, and as the children of the earth, bear your lilies to the upper light and the fragrance of spirituality will reward you for your toil. We shall breathe upon you the melodies of love until all things shall be fulfilled. Trust us!

The Guides.

THE ORDER OF THE WHITE ROSE

This mystic order is Rosicrucian in aim and is composed only of adepts in spiritual science and wisdom, only such as have mastered the four series of Teachings elsewhere described, which form the System of Philosophy Concerning Divinity, are eligible. Already the order numbers many in America and Europe; it will spread Westward and Eastward, and we encourage each one who enters the college as a student and who is afterward inspired to go on through the prescribed studies, however feeble and dormant to them their psychic powers may seem, to aspire and toil for adeptship. All such will receive the increasing fruitions of the order. To these, on the payment of the annual fee of five dollars, the publications of the order, including all Teachings, books and periodicals, shall be free.

For application to the order address J. C. F. Grumbine, 7820 Hawthorne ave., Station P, Chicago.

THE END